ARCHITECTS

OF THE UNITED STATES OF AMERICA

OF THE UNITED STATES OF AMERICA

ARCHITECTS

OF THE UNITED STATES OF AMERICA

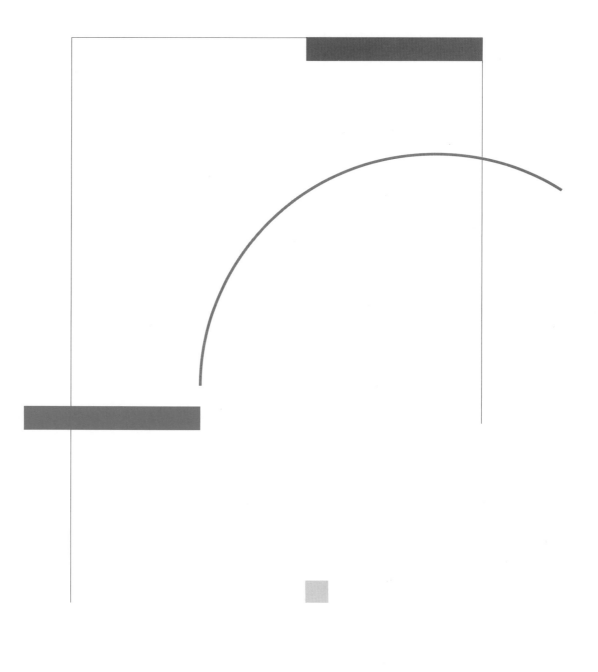

1 9 8 9 - 1 9 9 0

ISBN 0 9589598 7 0
© 1989
The Images Publishing Group
Melbourne, Australia 1989

CONTENTS

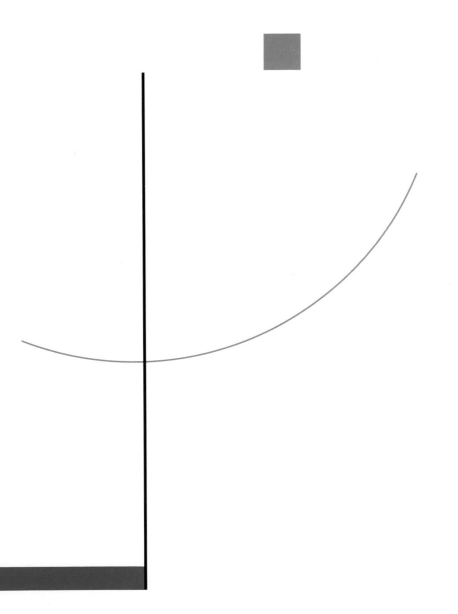

FOREWORD

To a large extent, our national character is expressed in the design of our homes, our cities and our towns. When we look at the structures we have erected around us, we see our past and our future. We see an evolution of thought and industry and style.

Our architecture expresses our pride in ourselves and our constant striving for new and better ways to approach the creation of space for increasingly complex uses.

No architectural form seems to capture the American spirit as much as the skyscraper. The drama of tall buildings seems to have struck a cord in most Americans. The impact these leviathans have had on the fabric of our cities and on our lives is profound. They have opened the door to new and different ways of working and living. They have sculpted our skylines and defined our cities. They ushered in the era of the corporate headquarters. And, they have presented us with the challenge of building better and better buildings that meet the criteria of modern tenants.

Many definitions exist of what is considered "good architecture". My own thinking is that well designed buildings are not only strong sculptural elements that appeal aesthetically, but are also buildings that enhance their environment and provide a pleasing working environment for tenants in terms of both form and function.

I have had the opportunity of working with many of the firms profiled in this volume. In each instance I entered the design process with the charge that the building stand the test of time. That it be looked upon proudly not only by my firm and the building's tenants, but also by the citizens of the city in which it stands.

More than 30 years ago when I began Gerald D. Hines Interests, it was not generally believed that excellence in design was a goal for which a developer could afford to reach. Today, time after time, in cities across the United States, we have proven that quality architecture, great architecture, is not only worth pursuing, it is a necessary ingredient in the overall success of a project.

I am proud to be included in this book which highlights the enormous talent and diversity of the American architectural community. Architecture is an exciting field, and the men and women that choose it as their profession are to be applauded and encouraged to bring to the field the very best they have to offer. I look forward to the challenges of the future and I hope someday future generations will look at the work we are doing today with pride and interest.

GERALD D. HINES

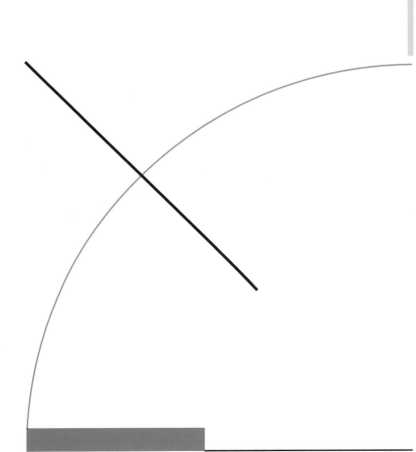

Right: Built in the early 1970s, The American Institute of Architects headquarters building was designed to wrap around the historic Octagon House and Museum. A quiet courtyard divides the two. The AIA building is currently undergoing a major renovation.

Below: The Octagon was built in 1801 as the Tayloe family residence, and has served as a private residence, a school, and multi-family housing. In 1902, the AIA purchased The Octagon, renovated it and used it as its headquarters until 1949.

THE AMERICAN INSTITUTE OF ARCHITECTS

"Architecture is the handwriting of man." Bernard Maybeck, Architect

B. Brewer, Jr.   S. Damianos   G. Hammond

G. Palermo   C. Smith   T. Eyerman

C.J. Lawler   J. Cramer

THE AMERICAN INSTITUTE OF ARCHITECTS

AIA National Headquarters
1735 New York Avenue, N.W.
Washington, DC 20006

TELEPHONE
(202) 626 7300

CABLE ADDRESS
AMINARCH

FACSIMILE
(202) 783 8247

MASTERSPEC
1 800 424 5080

INFORMATION CENTER
(202) 626 7554

OFFICERS
President
Benjamin E. Brewer Jr., FAIA

First Vice President
Sylvester Damianos, FAIA

Vice President
Gerald S. Hammond, AIA

Vice President
C. James Lawler, AIA

Vice President
Gregory S. Palermo, AIA

Secretary
Christopher J. Smith, AIA

Treasurer
Thomas J. Eyerman, FAIA,RIBA

Executive Vice President/CEO
James P. Cramer, Hon. AIA

EXECUTIVE MANAGEMENT COMMITTEE

Executive Vice President/
Chief Executive Officer
James P. Cramer, Hon. AIA

General Counsel
John DiNardo

Chief Financial Officer/COO
Fred DeLuca

Group Vice President - Education
James E. Ellison, FAIA

Group Vice President - Business
Steven A. Etkin

Group Vice President - Membership
Susan Hecht

Group Vice President - Design & Practice
James A. Scheeler, FAIA

Group Vice President - External Affairs
Gregg Ward

Since 1857, The American Institute of Architects has represented the professional interests of America's architects. Members of the AIA adhere to a Code of Ethics and Professional Conduct which assures the client, the public and colleagues of an architect's dedication to the highest standards in professional practice.

As members of the AIA, more than 53,000 architects express their own commitment to the highest standards in design and livability in our nation's buildings and cities. Though the AIA functions as a national organization, at its heart are almost 300 local and state organizations providing members with the essential local focus that reflects the nature of their professional lives.

The AIA, through its public outreach, education, and governmental affairs activities, works on behalf of a public environment that is responsive to the people it serves. The AIA encourages the development of well-designed, affordable housing for all Americans. Its Search for Shelter Program involves architects in coalitions with local community leaders to find solutions to the problems of homelessness and lack of housing in America's cities. The AIA supports efforts to create livable cities that are inviting, affirming expressions of community life through programs like its Regional/Urban Design Assistance Teams. The AIA's Vision 2000 program is a multi-year process designed to assess -- and ultimately shape -- the future of architecture, and, therefore, architectural practice. Its goal is to ensure that architects and the public they serve are prepared to create an environment that will serve the needs of society in the 21st Century.

Through the AIA, America's architects are working with public officials to improve the nation's built and natural environments. By speaking with a united voice, architects in the AIA can influence government decisions that affect the practice of the profession and quality of American life. The Institute constantly monitors legislative and regulatory actions and uses the collective power of its membership to influence decisions being made by federal, state, and local policy makers.

The Institute's nationally recognized awards programs set the standard for architectural excellence while cultivating an ever-growing audience for good design. The AIA Fellowship Program recognizes those members who have made notable contributions to the advancement of the profession.

'Architecture', the AIA's award-winning monthly magazine, features complete coverage of building technology and professional practice, and highlights architectural achievement.

The Institute serves its members with professional development opportunities, contract documents, information services, personal benefits, and client-oriented resources. Contract documents developed and revised by the AIA are the model for the design and construction industry. The AIA's members take part in committees at work on historic resources, design, interiors, practice management, regional and urban development, building performance and regulations, energy, and housing. Committees on architecture for health, justice, education, and aging are the focus of new ideas and responses. To aid younger professionals, the Intern-Architect Development Program, registration-exam preparation courses, and employment referral services are frequently offered by local chapters.

The AIA strives to meet the needs and interests of the nation's architects and the public they serve by developing public awareness of the value of architecture and the importance of good design.

Above: Built in 1801 as the Tayloe family residence, The Octagon became the presidential mansion for President James Madison and his wife Dolley when the White House was burned during the War of 1812. The Octagon Museum today is an accredited museum administered by the American Architectural Foundation.

Right: Dr. Lynn V. Cheney, left, chairman, National Endowment for the Humanities, and James P. Cramer, past president of the American Architectural Foundation, teach a history lesson on the lives of James and Dolley Madison to a class of sixth graders at The Octagon.

THE AMERICAN ARCHITECTURAL FOUNDATION AT THE OCTAGON

T. Eyerman   N.L. Koonce

THE AMERICAN ARCHITECTURAL FOUNDATION AT THE OCTAGON

1735 New York Avenue, N.W.
Washington, DC 20006
Telephone: (202) 626 7500
Cable: AMINARCH
Facsimile: (202) 783 8247
The Octagon
1799 New York Avenue, N.W.
Washington, DC 20006
Director
Nancy Davis
Telephone: (202) 638 3221
Hours:
Tuesday-Friday, 10 am.-4 pm.
Saturday-Sunday, Noon-4 pm.
Closed Mondays

BOARD OF REGENTS

Thomas J. Eyerman, FAIA, RIBA
- Chairman
Norman L. Koonce, FAIA
- President
L. William Chapin, II, AIA
- Secretary-Treasurer
Terrence M. McDermott,
- Vice Chairman
Regents:
Harold L. Adams,FAIA
Richard G. Boxall
John H. Burgee, FAIA
Philip W. Dinsmore, FAIA
Mildred Friedman, Hon. AIA
Elliott S. Hall
Lou Harris
Helmut Jahn, FAIA
Lloyd Kaiser
Allan S. Kaplan
Karl J. Krapek
Bill Lacy, FAIA
Alan J. Lockman
Susan Maxman, AIA
Thomas L. McKittrick, FAIA
John K. Mott, FAIA
Ted P. Pappas, FAIA
Philip W. Pillsbury, Jr.
Jay A. Pritzker
Robert A.M. Stern, FAIA

AIA COLLEGE OF FELLOWS EXECUTIVE COMMITTEE

Chancellor
Preston M. Bolton, FAIA
Vice Chancellor
William A. Rose Jr., FAIA
Secretary
Robert B. Marquis, FAIA
Bursar
L. Jane Hastings, FAIA
Senior Executive
James A. Scheeler, FAIA

OFFICERS, AMERICAN ARCHITECTURAL FOUNDATION

President
Norman L. Koonce, FAIA
Vice President
Raymond P. Rhinehart

The American Architectural Foundation at The Octagon works to advance the cause of excellence in American architecture by serving as a link between the public and this country's architects. It fulfills this mission by advocating creative and responsible public stewardship of America's architectural heritage: sponsoring alliances between the public and America's architects; and fostering development of a national vision of livable communities through design excellence.

Established in 1942 by The American Institute of Architects, the Foundation advances the cause of excellence in American architecture by stimulating the public's awareness and understanding of the world we create. Recognizing that it is the public, even more than design professionals, that ultimately has the power to shape our surroundings, the Foundation fosters a broad range of programs committed to the ideal of an informed public prepared to become stewards of their communities. Major components of this effort include:

Education

The Foundation and the AIA together develop materials for classroom activities that teach elementary and high school students about architecture and the design process. In the past five years, the Foundation's scholarship program has awarded nearly $1 million to future architects in colleges across the United States and Canada. Other educational programs include major symposia, lectures, and conferences offered to scholars, the public, and the design professional.

The Octagon

Headquarters and symbol of The American Architectural Foundation, The Octagon is a designated National Historic Landmark open to the public and the oldest museum in America dedicated to architecture. Each year thousands of visitors tour its period rooms and take part in the special programs that commemorate the cultural and historical events that have occurred in The Octagon.

Exhibitions

During the past 10 years, more than 80 exhibitions have been mounted on architecture, design, and the decorative arts. The Traveling Exhibition Program offers a varied selection of exhibitions to libraries, historical societies, and museums across the country and abroad.

Publications

The Foundation has developed an extensive series of publications aimed at a general audience as well as scholars. Recent publications such as 'The Architecture of Richard Morris Hunt' and 'The Architect and the British Country House' provide innovative scholarly research for the field.

Prints and Drawings Collection

Internationally recognized as an outstanding repository and invaluable body of visual material documenting architecture from the late 19th century to the present, the collection is an important scholarly resource.

Pursuing its commitment to serve as the link between the American public and architecture, the Foundation offers a wide range of public membership categories, both for the general public and for corporations. For additional information, please contact:
The American Architectural Foundation, 1735 New York Avenue, N.W., Washington, D.C. 20006, U.S.A.

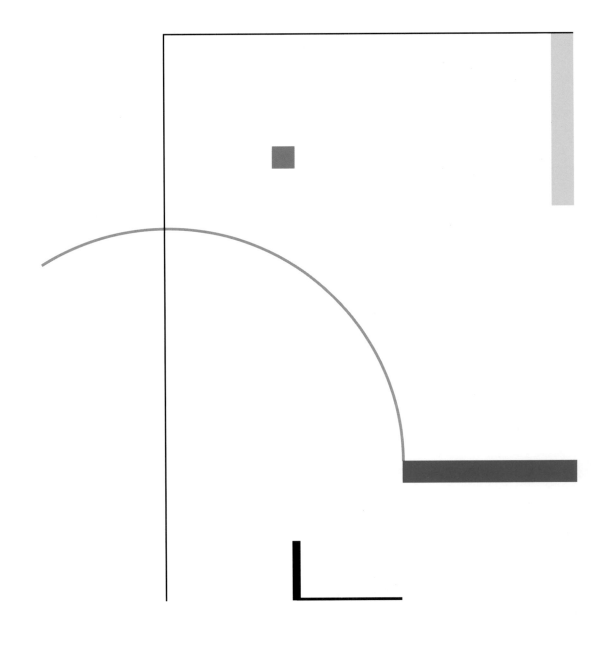

ARCHITECTS

ARCHITECTS

adache
associates
architects p.a.

1

2

3

4

5

6

1. Port de Plaisance, St. Maarten, Netherland Antilles
2. Art Institute of Fort Lauderdale, FL
3. Mr. Laffs, Fort Lauderdale, FL
4. One University Drive, Fort Lauderdale, FL
5. Sogebank, Port au Prince, Haiti
6. Ramada Inn, Curacao, Netherland Antilles

ADACHE ASSOCIATES ARCHITECTS, P.A.

D. Adache

G. Winne   G. Fletcher

L. Barrera   O. Garcia

ADACHE ASSOCIATES ARCHITECTS, P.A.

ESTABLISHED
June 1969

ADDRESSES
550 South Federal Highway
Fort Lauderdale, FL 33301
Telephone (305) 525 8133
Facsimile (305) 728 8159

Satellite Office
7 King Street
Christiansted, St. Croix
U.S. Virgin Islands
Telephone (809) 778 7885

Affiliate Office
One Design Center, Inc.
2828 Lawndale Drive
P.O. Box 29426
Greensboro, NC 27429
Telephone (919) 288 0134

PRINCIPAL
Daniel E. Adache, A.I.A. Architect

ASSOCIATES
George Winne, A.I.A. Architect
- Vice President
George Fletcher
- Vice President, Production
Louis Barrera, Architect
- Production Coordinator
Oscar Garcia, Architect
- Director of Design

NUMBER OF EMPLOYEES
32

REGISTRATION
National Council of Architectural
Registration Boards
Florida, California, Washington,
Pennsylvania, New Jersey, Ohio,
Connecticut, North Carolina, U.S.
Virgin Islands, District of Columbia.

POINT OF CONTACT
Daniel E. Adache - President
James Caruso - Marketing Director

PROJECT TYPES
Hotel, Hospitality & Resort
Residential
Commercial
Recreational
Retail
Educational
Health & Medical
Civic

SERVICES
Architectural
Construction Management
Interior Design & Space Planning
Concept Development
Budget Management
Master Planning
Programming
Governmental Approvals
Computer Aided Design
Renovation

CURRENT AND RECENT PROJECTS

Hospitality & Resort
Port de Plaisance, St. Maarten,
Netherland Antilles
Ramada Inn, Curacao, Netherland Antilles
Diamond Keturah Stouffers Resort, St.
Croix, U.S. Virgin Islands
Inverrary Resort, Fort Lauderdale, FL
Berkley Inn, Fort Lauderdale, FL
Coakley Bay Resort, St. Croix,
U.S. Virgin Islands
Antigua Grand Hotel, Dickinson Bay,
Antigua

Residential
Cormorant Cove Condominiums, St. Croix,
U.S. Virgin Islands
Frenchmans Cove Condominiums,
St. Thomas, U.S. Virgin Islands
Pond Apple Creek Apartments,
Fort Lauderdale, FL
Highland Place, Coral Springs, FL
Ocean Club Condominiums, Boca Raton, FL

Commercial
One University Drive, Fort Lauderdale, FL
Sogebank, Port au Prince, Haiti
Caribank, Fort Lauderdale, FL
STP Headquarters, Fort Lauderdale, FL

PROFILE AND PHILOSOPHY
The firm of Adache Associates Architects,
P.A. has maintained a consistent record of
performance since the firm's establishment
in 1969. The Adache team has
demonstrated a wide range of leadership
capabilities in management of the design
process, in the control of project costs and
schedules, in energy conservation
methodology and design excellence.

It is the philosophy of the firm to maintain
the client as an integral part of the design
team. The client remains intimately
involved to varying degrees throughout all
phases of the project.

Architecture combines creativity and
technology in order to provide form and
function for the built environment.

Innovative design is a result of the talent
who created it and is a prerequisite for
quality architecture. Aesthetics is not only
the result of creativity, but also the
economics of efficiency and longevity
as well.

Because quality of design ultimately
determines the value of property, quality
architecture creates a successful project by
minimizing financial risk while maximizing
real estate investments.

The Adache team is a carefully selected,
experienced and well managed group of
award winning architects who take pride in
their numerous recognized awards and
accomplishments. Since 1976 the firm has
received 17 design awards from peer groups
on a national, state and local level.

The challenge of meeting today's design
needs demands advanced technical
knowledge. Facing the challenge, the
Adache team, in addition to the recognized
technical staff, offers Computer Aided
Design and Drafting (CADD), a system with
the most current and modern equipment
available on the market. CADD services the
needs of our clients by enhancing several
areas such as: speed, accuracy, legibility,
presentation of drawings and CADD
telecommunications.

HOTEL, HOSPITALITY & RESORT DIVISION
While the firm of Adache Associates
Architects has a wide range of experience in
many building types, its Hotel, Hospitality
and Resort division has developed into one
of the most respected and recognized hotel
architectural firms. In addition to the many
years of experience and the many hospitality
projects, the firm has its in-house hotel
management consultant, James Caruso.
The firm is affiliated with One Design
Center, Inc. of Greensboro, NC, one of the
country's leading Hospitality Interior Design
Firms.

Capital Professional Centre

National Institutes of Health

Office: Interior Design & Space Planning

Aquinas College

Chinatown Archway

AEPA ARCHITECTS ENGINEERS, P.C.

Alfred H. Liu, AIA

AEPA ARCHITECTS ENGINEERS, P.C.

ESTABLISHED DATE
1976

ADDRESS
2421 Pennsylvania Ave
Washington, DC 20037

TELEPHONE
(202) 822 8320

FACSIMILE
(202) 457 0908

PRESIDENT
Alfred H. Liu, AIA

DIRECTORS
Paul Jarvis, P.E. - Strategic Planning
C.M. Liu, M.B.A. - Operations
Dwan Tai, Ph.D. - Development

NUMBER OF EMPLOYEES
60

PROJECT TYPES
Commercial/Offices/Retail/
Hotels
Health/Biomedical/Animal
Labs
Urban Design/Landscape
Design
Educational/Research Labs
Renovation
Multi-Family/Residential
Feasibility Studies/Master
Planning

DISCIPLINES
Architecture
Construction Administration
Space Planning
Interior Design
Electrical Engineering
Mechanical Engineering
Structural Engineering
Computer Aided Design
(CADD)

PROJECTS/CLIENTS
Far East Trade Center
National Institutes of Health
Environmental Protection Agency
Techworld
Andrews Air Force Base
US AID
International Developers, Inc.
St. Elizabeth's Hospital
Veteran's Administration Medical Center
Capital Professional Center
Aquinas College
US Department of Commerce
US Department of the Army
US Department of the Navy
DC Government
Grand Rapids Jr. College
Crescent Construction
Peabody Apartments
Media Tech Plaza
Antioch Apartments
Mitre Corporation
Melvin Simon & Associates, Inc.
Potomac Electric Power Company
Washington Realty Group
North Gallery Place Associates
National Corporation of Housing
Partnership
Quadrangle Corporation
The Evans Company
Pacific United Ltd.
Cumberland Corporation

THE PRACTICE & PHILOSOPHY

Creative achievements and design awards best publicize the unique capabilities of AEPA, a full-service, 60-person design firm of architects; mechanical, electrical, civil and structural engineers; planners; interior designers; landscape architects; and construction administrators. AEPA is currently in the process of establishing a presence in New York City, Puerto Rico and the Far East, in addition to offices in D.C. and Maryland.

Health care facilities design is a major speciality of AEPA; within the past decade, our principal architects and engineers have designed more than two dozen health care facilities both in the United States and abroad. These projects have ranged from major Federal contracts with the National Institutes of Health and the U.S. Public Health Service to university and private hospital/medical facilities.

Office and commercial building design is also a major focus for AEPA. We work closely with our clients to insure that our designs accommodate all elements such as commercial/financial viability; market attraction; customer/client ambience; environment and zoning constraints; and site and landscape planning to accommodate community concerns and parking and access needs.

Our philosophy focuses on achieving our clients' objectives; ranging from simple, traditional buildings to creating more innovative "works of architectural art" that can serve as unique showplaces to attract customers and enhance community pride. AEPA designed the Far East Trade Center, a 1.2 million square foot, $200 million mixed-use complex in the heart of Washington's Chinatown, the largest Asian-oriented project in the Western Hemisphere. Another recent project was a 153-unit high-rise apartment building in Washington, D.C. On a smaller scale, AEPA's headquarters makes its own mark as a distinctive office/commercial building.

Design plays a critical role in meeting the interrelated functional needs of our clients. Sensitivity to and awareness of such needs by the AEPA project team, together with the latest computer technology, results in design solutions that are cost-efficient and contribute to the objectives of the client.

1

2

3

5

4

6

1. Figueroa at Wilshire Tower, Los Angeles, CA
2. GTE Regional Headquarters
   (formerly Prudential Western Regional HQ),
   Thousand Oaks, CA
3. Satellite Parking/Office/Child Day Care
   Project, Los Angeles, CA
4. 865 South Figueroa Tower, Los Angeles, CA
5. Home Savings of America Tower,
   Los Angeles, CA
6. ARCO Plaza and Towers, Los Angeles, CA

C. Martin   D. Martin

ALBERT C. MARTIN AND ASSOCIATES

Planning Architecture Engineering
Interiors

ESTABLISHED

1906

ADDRESS

811 West Seventh Street
Los Angeles, CA 90017

TELEPHONE

(213) 683 1900

FACSIMILE

(213) 614 6002

PARTNERS

Christopher C. Martin, AIA
- Managing Partner
David C. Martin, AIA
- Partner in Charge of Design
Albert C. Martin, FAIA
J. Edward Martin, FASCE

PRINCIPALS

Robert W. Braunschweiger,
- General Manager
Gustav H. Ullner, AIA
Herbert G. Winkler, SE
Donald K. Toy, AIA
Gilbert W. Thweatt, AIA
John H. Johnson III, AIA
Richard A. Halfon, PE
Nabih Youssef, PE
Aram Tatikian

AVERAGE NUMBER OF EMPLOYEES

200

ADDITIONAL OFFICES

Irvine, CA
Tokyo, Japan

HISTORY

In 1904, Albert C. Martin brought his family to a city that was not much more than open expanses of land and with miles of coastline and a feel of the desert. But fresh from his architecture and engineering studies at the University of Illinois, young A.C., as he was known to his friends, saw something else in the tranquil landscape: the potential for growth.

With his vision of the future in mind, A.C. founded Albert C. Martin and Associates (ACMA) in 1906, an architecture and engineering firm. Over the past eight decades, perhaps no other design firm has so greatly contributed to the remarkable growth of the built environment in Southern California.

If the senior Martin revolutionized techniques in construction, engineering, and design, his sons, Albert C. Martin Jr. and J. Edward Martin, put those skills to work in building the now fast growing metropolis of Southern California. When Al and Ed Martin took charge of the firm in 1945, skyscrapers were beginning to appear on the horizon and cars on the first freeways, and the population swelled into the millions.

Albert C. Martin and Associates now designed buildings to meet the needs of Southern California's growing population and rapidly developing high-tech industries. Under Al and Ed's leadership, the firm grew and developed a strong expertise in both architecture and building engineering.

David C. Martin and Christopher C. Martin, sons of Al and Ed respectively, continue today to lead Albert C. Martin and Associates in the tradition of their fathers and grandfather: offering clients the highest level of professional service available. Each brings special talents and a unique personality to the firm.

The long standing image of the ACMA as a stable, yet constantly evolving presence in the architecture and engineering community provides the foundation for the firm's new creative direction. The youthful, energetic management styles of Christopher and David encourage expansive thinking and allow a blend of traditional and contemporary ideas.

PHILOSOPHY AND PROJECT APPROACH

The third generation of Martins continue to be guided by the foundations originally set forth by A.C., Sr. over 80 years ago. Albert C. Martin and Associates today represents a new balance of talent, style and attitude, bonded by the same commitment to quality and service to the client initially made by A.C. in the early years of the Century, and carried through to today by Al and Ed Martin.

A company does not survive through three generations without a solid foundation and committed family. Not only is there a very special family tie within Albert C. Martin and Associates; there is also unusual company dedication. Many of the firm's Principals and Associates have been with the firm for 20 years or more; generations of the same family continue with the firm. All this history, coupled with a flexible and forward-looking approach, adds up to a firm with the wealth of experience and vision necessary to meet the ever-changing challenges of building and rebuilding of one of the most vital regions in the world.

In this high-tech age, a successful architecture and engineering project demands the support of specialists: architects; structural, mechanical, electrical and civil engineers; experts on interiors; experienced planners and draftsmen. With our multi-service capability, ACMA can assist clients on any level, offering them any or all of the full spectrum of services provided by our firm.

A different approach for a different generation - - with the development process becoming more complex than ever, only a multi-service firm has the capability to assist its clients every step of the way.

BOHLIN POWELL LARKIN CYWINSKI

Directors (L-R): J. Larkin, P. Bohlin, R. Powell and B. Cywinski

BOHLIN POWELL LARKIN CYWINSKI
Architecture Planning
Interior Design

ESTABLISHED DATE
1965

ADDRESSES
Wilkes-Barre
182 North Franklin Street
Wilkes-Barre, PA 18701
Telephone (717) 825 8756
Facsimile (717) 825 3744

Pittsburgh
307 Fourth Avenue
Pittsburgh, PA 15222
Telephone (412) 765 3890
Facsimile (412) 765 2209

Philadelphia
125 South Ninth Street
Philadelphia, PA 19107
Telephone (215) 592 0600
Facsimile (215) 592 9637

DIRECTORS/PRINCIPALS
Peter Q. Bohlin, FAIA
Richard E. Powell, AIA
John F. Larkin, AIA
Bernard J. Cywinski, AIA

NUMBER OF EMPLOYEES
50

PROJECT TYPES
Corporate Facilities
Educational Buildings
Industrial Buildings
Public Buildings
Recreation/Sports Facilities
Restoration/Adaptive Reuse
Health Care Facilities

OTHER DISCIPLINES
Urban Design
Master Planning
Programming
Space Planning
Interior Design
Furniture Design

PERSONS TO CONTACT
Wilkes-Barre
Peter Q. Bohlin, FAIA
Richard E. Powell, AIA
Pittsburgh
Jon C. Jackson, AIA
Philadelphia
John F. Larkin, AIA
Bernard J. Cywinski, AIA

CURRENT/RECENT PROJECTS
Corporate Headquarters Addition,
Rochester & Pittsburgh Coal Company

Corporate Headquarters,
InterMetro Industries

Corporate Headquarters,
Royal Oil and Gas Company

Comprehensive Plan, Office and Dining
Building, Advanced Tactical Fighter
Building, Westinghouse Defense and
Electronics Center, Westinghouse
Electric Corporation

Offices, Laboratories and Elevator Testing
Tower, Westinghouse Elevator Corporation

Orphans Court and Domestic Affairs Agency
Office Building, Luzerne County, PA

Software Engineering Institute, Carnegie
Mellon University

Center for Computer Aids for Industrial
Productivity, Rutgers University

Biotechnology and Bioengineering Center,
University of Pittsburgh

Engineering and Science Building, Behrend
College, Pennsylvania State University

Regional Shopping Mall,
The Rouse Company

Street Furniture and Infrastructure Study,
Three Rivers Stadium Master Plan,
Washington's Landing Development Master
Plan, City of Pittsburgh

Passenger Terminal, Harrisburg
International Airport

H. Douglas Barclay Law Library,
Syracuse University

Knott Athletic, Recreation and Convocation
Center, Mount Saint Mary's College

Carnivore Exhibit, Master Plan and
Facilities Planning Manual, Philadelphia
Zoological Garden

Hockey Arena and Student Center,
Clarkson University

Judge Advocate General's School,
University of Virginia

Outpatient Clinic,
Geisinger Medical Center

PHILOSOPHY/HISTORY

Background
Bohlin Powell Larkin Cywinski has
practiced architecture and planning since
1965 and now has three Pennsylvania
offices: Wilkes-Barre, Pittsburgh and
Philadelphia. Geographically, the firm's
work ranges from Virginia north through
New England and west to Ohio. Organized
as a professional corporation, the firm has
four principals and seven associates with a
total staff of approximately 50. Since the
firm's inception a reputation has developed
for innovative and outstanding design
excellence. The more than 75 awards
earned by the firm and the extensive
publication of its work by foreign and
domestic journals attest to the high regard
in which its work is held.

Service
The firm offers clients a range of services
beyond the general practice of architecture.
BPLC regularly provides feasibility studies,
master planning, programming, space
planning, interior design, site design,
landscape design, historic surveys,
preservation/restoration services and
energy analysis using staff personnel with
particular skills in those areas. These
activities are not simple adjuncts to
traditional architectural services; they are
often crucial to the solution of a client's
design problem and become the generators
of a project's exceptional qualities.

Skills
Combinations of the services and staff
member skills mentioned above qualify the
firm for demanding assignments dealing
with complex problems, difficult sites,
extraordinary budget and time constraints,
unusual technological requirements, and
intricate integrations of new construction
with existing buildings and contexts.

Philosophy of Problem Solving
Much of the firm's design reputation is built
on synergistic solutions to multiple
technical concerns. BPLC's problem
solving approach emphasizes thorough
research and orderly analysis of each
project's unique technical, economic and
human circumstances. The firm's concern
for the right solution and for good design is
neither superficial nor limited to aesthetics.
BPLC's design process seeks a well
balanced response to all pertinent realities of
each situation and project, while
implementing solutions with a consistently
high and detailed level of technical care.

Photo Credit: Richard Payne, AIA

Photo Credit: Richard Payne, AIA

Photo Credit: Richard Payne, AIA

Photo Credit: Richard Payne, AIA

Photo Credit: T.A. Trimbur, courtesy PPG Industries

Photo Credit: Copyright 1988/Rion Rizzo/Creative Sources/Atlanta

Top: Pennzoil Place, Houston.
Bottom: Transco Tower and Park, Houston.

Top: AT&T Corporate Headquarters,
New York City.
Bottom: PPG Corporate Headquarters,
Pittsburgh.

Top: RepublicBank Center, Houston.
Bottom: IBM Tower at Atlantic Place, Atlanta.

JOHN BURGEE ARCHITECTS

John Burgee (3rd left) and partners Stephen Achilles (left) and K. Jeffries Sydness (2nd right) with design consultant Philip Johnson (center) and the associates of John Burgee Architects

JOHN BURGEE ARCHITECTS

DATE ESTABLISHED
Partnership formed in 1967 as Philip Johnson and John Burgee, Architects

ADDRESS
885 Third Avenue
New York, NY 10022-4802

TELEPHONE
(212) 751 7440

FACSIMILE
(212) 751 7449

PARTNERS
John Burgee
Stephen Achilles
K. Jeffries Sydness

ASSOCIATES
John Manley
Laurie Levinson
J. David Harrison
Donald M. Porter

DESIGN CONSULTANT
Philip Johnson

NUMBER OF EMPLOYEES
70

PROJECT TYPES
Commercial
Mixed-use
Institutional
Educational
Cultural
Religious
Residential
Retail

RECENT AND CURRENT PROJECTS
IDS Center, Minneapolis
Pennzoil Place, Houston
National Center for the Performing Arts, Bombay, India
Dade County Cultural Center, Miami
AT&T Corporate Headquarters, New York City
101 California, San Francisco
PPG Corporate Headquarters, Pittsburgh
Transco Tower and Park, Houston
The New Cleveland Playhouse, Cleveland
RepublicBank Center, Houston
580 California, San Francisco
53rd At Third, New York City
Momentum Place, Dallas
Tycon Towers, Vienna, Virginia
International Place, Boston
500 Boylston Street, Boston
190 South LaSalle Street, Chicago
IBM Tower at Atlantic Center, Atlanta
Times Square Center, New York City
One Ninety One Peachtree Tower, Atlanta
Canadian Broadcast Centre, Toronto
343 Sansome Street, San Francisco
The Museum of Broadcasting, New York City
PortAmerica, Prince Georges County, Maryland
Puerta de Europa, Madrid

FIRM PROFILE
John Burgee Architects has been associated with buildings whose innovative designs have exerted significant influence over the course of twentieth-century architecture.

From the opening of Philip Johnson's office in the 1940's through the formation of the John Burgee-Philip Johnson partnership in 1967 to the present, the firm has been instrumental in instigating major evolutionary turns in architecture.

The firm's designs have become the focus of public and professional attention and have been cited as major achievements in the field of architecture. While Burgee and Johnson designs exhibit strong and distinctive characters, one building usually bears no resemblance to the next.

John Burgee Architects has been responsible for introducing advances and innovations within existing building technology. Its technical expertise, derived from decades of production-oriented experience on complicated high-rise structures, has translated into efficient structures of lasting quality.

John Burgee Architects is now under the leadership of partners John Burgee, Stephen Achilles and K. Jeffries Sydness. Philip Johnson acts as design consultant to the firm. Four associates -- John Manley, Laurie Levinson, J. David Harrison and Donald M. Porter -- and a professional staff of 70 comprise the office of John Burgee Architects.

While the firm has designed structures for many different clients, it is noted for having established long-term alliances with several of the country's leading development concerns, including Gerald D. Hines Interests, Prentiss Properties, James T. Lewis Enterprises, Park Tower Realty, and The John Buck Company.

The buildings created through these partnerships proved that quality design hampered neither the economic viability nor the functional capability of a development; in fact, it demonstrated it to be an asset, enriching the built environment while contributing to the success of projects in highly competitive real estate markets.

The strong rapport developed between John Burgee Architects and its clients is based on how the firm is structured. The size and workload of the office is limited to allow close, personal participation by Mr. Burgee and his partners on each project on a daily basis. A team of partners, associates, and staff architects is established at the outset of each project, all of whom remain involved from the design phase through construction.

This strong sense of participation and continuity results in completed projects of the highest quality, where the specific individual requirements of use, site, budget, location, and context are met, and an extraordinarily high level of design clarity and detail is achieved.

At present, the office of John Burgee Architects has millions of square feet of space in various stages of design and construction in the United States, Australia, Canada and Europe.

1. Cambridge Seven Associates, Inc., 1050 Massachusetts Avenue, Cambridge, MA
2. Harrah's Boardwalk Hotel and Casino, Atlantic City, NJ
3. Digital Equipment Corporation, Spitbrook Engineering Facility, Nashua, NH
4. INNOVA, Houston, TX
5. INNOVA, Houston, TX
6. Riverfront Office Park, Cambridge, MA
7. Charles Hotel, Cambridge, MA
8. Courtyard of Charles Square, Mixed-use Development, Cambridge, MA
9. United Technologies Corporation Conference Center, EPCOT Living Seas Pavilion, Orlando, FL
10. Rarities Restaurant, Charles Hotel, Cambridge, MA
11. JG Furniture Systems Showroom, International Design Center of New York, Long Island City, NY
12. NBC Bank Plaza, San Antonio, TX
13. General Cinema, Town East Theater, Mesquite, TX
14. The Talbot's Inc., Corporate Headquarters, Hingham, MA
15. The Talbot's Inc., Corporate Offices, Hingham, MA

CAMBRIDGE SEVEN ASSOCIATES, INC.

Principals Back (L-R): G. Rankine, R. Baker,
P. Chermayeff, P. Dietrich, G. Johnson,
J. Stebbins, B. Poole. Front (L-R): R. Tuve,
P. Sollogub, C. Redmon and P. Kuttner

CAMBRIDGE SEVEN ASSOCIATES, INC.

ESTABLISHED DATE
1962

ADDRESSES
1050 Massachusetts Avenue
Cambridge, MA 02138
Telephone (617) 492 7000
Facsimile   (617) 492 7007

Affiliated Office
Cambridge Seven Associates, Inc./
Chermayeff and Geismar
15 East 26th Street
New York, NY 10010
Telephone (212) 889 4220

DIRECTORS
Louis Bakanowsky, FAIA
Ronald Baker, AIA
Ivan Chermayeff, FAIGA
Peter Chermayeff, FAIA
Paul Dietrich, FAIA
Thomas Geismar, FAIGA
Gary Johnson, AIA
Peter Kuttner, AIA
Bobby Poole, AIA
G.W. Terry Rankine, FAIA
Charles Redmon, FAIA
Peter Sollogub
John Stebbins, AIA
Richard Tuve, AIA

NUMBER OF EMPLOYEES
75

PROJECT TYPES
Mixed-use Developments
Corporate and Speculative Office
 Buildings
Retail Facilities
Museum/Visitor Centers
Aquariums
Transportation Facilities
Educational Facilities
Convention Center/Arena Facilities

DISCIPLINES
Architecture
Interior Design
Graphic Design
Exhibit Design
Industrial Design
Urban Design
Master Planning
Programming

PERSON TO CONTACT
Charles Redmon
- Managing Principal

CURRENT AND RECENT PROJECTS

Office and Corporate Facilities
Charles Square, Cambridge, MA
$60m mixed-use development

NBC Bank Plaza, San Antonio, TX
$50m, 35-story, 500,000²f office tower

Northeast Technology Center III,
Shrewsbury, MA
Digital Equipment Corporation
$19m, 400,000²f office and research

Riverfront Office Park, Cambridge, MA
$58m, 15 and 20-story office towers

The Talbots, Inc., Hingham, MA
$9m, 126,000²f corporate headquarters

Spitbrook Engineering Facility, Nashua, NH
Digital Equipment Corporation
$10m, 200,000²f engineering facility

IBM Glendale, Glendale, NY
$15m Office and Laboratory Facility

Hotel Projects
The Charles Hotel, Cambridge, MA
$20m, 330-room luxury hotel

Logan Airport Hilton Hotel, Boston, MA
Renovation and Addition
$40m, 725-room luxury hotel

Harrah's Boardwalk Hotel and Casino
Atlantic City, NJ
$88m, 600-room casino hotel

Sheraton Center Renovation, New York, NY
$3.4m renovation

Holiday Inn/Crown Plaza, Boston, MA
$30m, 500-room hotel

(Compri) Hotels (prototype design)
Doubletree Corporation
175-200 rooms

Quail Springs Hotel, Oklahoma City, OK
(master plan and design) $15m, 300-room hotel

Retail Projects
Pavilions at Buckland Hills
Manchester, CT $20m, 900,000²f shopping mall

Franklin Mills, Philadelphia, PA
$35m, 2,000,000²f shopping mall

Innova, Houston, TX, Houston Design
Center $30m, 500,000²f showroom facility

Shops at Charles Square, Cambridge, MA
$3m, 40,000²f specialty shops

General Cinema Theaters Design,
Nationwide, Prototype design development

Osaka Marketplace, Osaka, Japan
$30m, 150,000²f festival market

Space Planning/Interior Design
Shearson Hammill, Nationwide
for Shearson Hammill & Company

Conference Center, Orlando, FL
Epcot Living Seas Pavilion
for United Technologies Corporation

DC 10 Interior Design
for McDonnell-Douglas Corporation

Furniture Showroom, Long Island City, NY
International Design Center of NY
for J.G. Furniture Systems

PROFILE AND BACKGROUND
Cambridge Seven Associates is based in Cambridge, Massachusetts with a staff of seventy-five people, including thirty-five registered architects. An affiliated graphic design office, Chermayeff & Geismar, is located in New York.

The Firm was founded in 1962 and is recognized internationally for innovative work in architecture, urban design, exhibitions and graphic, interior and industrial design. Cambridge Seven Associates has received numerous awards from national, state and local organizations for its efforts to pursue fresh and innovative solutions to often ordinary aspects of the built environment.

Cambridge Seven Associates provides its clients with a complete range of design services from initial feasibility studies through construction administration and post-occupancy evaluations. Although the base of the firm's practice is architectural design, our diverse experience includes urban design and planning, exhibit and graphic design, film production, audio-visual presentations, marketing brochures and product design.

APPROACH
Since its beginning, Cambridge Seven Associates has been guided by the conviction that a well-designed environment enriches the human experience. Underlying this attitude toward design is the belief that each assignment, at any scale, is an opportunity to apply fresh thinking in a search for appropriate solutions to problems. Successful results require objectivity and a willingness to listen and respond to the clients' needs and aspirations.

Cambridge Seven Associates is organized in such a way that each project team, through its key personnel, can draw upon a wide range of specialized internal disciplines as project resources. The principal-in-charge, whose overview is continuous for each project, is assisted by discipline directors, also principals of the firm, who focus on project management, planning and architectural design, technical standards/cost control, interior and exhibit design, and construction administration.

Quality and efficiency of our work has been recently enhanced by the fact that many of our design and production drawings are now produced with an in-house CADD system. This network of computers enables our staff to review efficiently design options and to achieve a consistent standard of detailing and documentation within effective project cost control parameters.

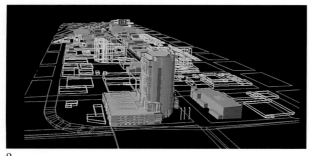

1

2

3

4

5

1. The Park, Brookline, MA
2. Olympic West Design Competition,
   Los Angeles, CA
3. The Pavilion at Park Square, Boston, MA
4. Commonwealth Flats, Boston, MA
5. 399 Boylston Street, Boston, MA

CBT/CHILDS BERTMAN TSECKARES & CASENDINO INC.

CBT/CHILDS BERTMAN TSECKARES & CASENDINO INC.

ESTABLISHED DATE
1967

ADDRESS
306 Dartmouth Street
Boston, MA 02116

TELEPHONE
(617) 262 4354

FACSIMILE
(617) 236 0378

DIRECTORS
Maurice F. Childs, AIA
Richard J. Bertman, FAIA
Charles N. Tseckares, FAIA
Anthony B. Casendino, ASLA

NUMBER OF EMPLOYEES
110

PROJECT TYPES
Commercial
Hospitality
Institutional
Interiors
Residential
Urban Design

OTHER DISCIPLINES
Architecture
Urban Design and
Landscape Architecture
Space Planning and
Interior Architecture

PERSON TO CONTACT
Charles N. Tseckares, FAIA
- Principal

CURRENT PROJECTS

Commercial

399 Boylston Street, Boston, MA
A thirteen-story, 250,000 square foot office building clad in masonry on the lower eight floors and reflective glass on the upper stories.

116 Huntington Avenue, Boston, MA
A twelve-story, 300,000 square foot office tower in Boston's historic Back Bay district.

Key Bank, Augusta, ME
An 85,000 square foot bank headquarters which symbolizes the revitalization of Maine's capital city.

73 Tremont Street, Boston, MA
A 350,000 square foot office building which received renovations and two major additions, and now features a rich marble lobby and a two-story penthouse crowned by an ornate copper dome.

Hospitality

Mount Washington Hotel and Resort, Bretton Woods, NH
The renovation of an historic hotel, including restoration of 155 first-class rooms and all public spaces, with a spectacular location in New Hampshire's White Mountain National Park.

Institutional

Montshire Museum of Science, Norwich, VT
A natural science museum which encompasses 70 acres along the Connecticut River, and offers both indoor and outdoor interactive exhibits.

Tufts University/Aidekman Arts Center, Medford, MA
A new arts complex integrating three existing buildings with 40,000 square feet of new construction to create a center for all arts curricula.

Interiors

Brown, Rudnick, Freed & Gesmer, Boston, MA
Downtown law offices encompassing three floors and 72,000 square feet of prime office space in a major Boston high-rise.

Dean Witter Reynolds, Northeast Region
Design of twenty-five branch offices throughout New England, New York and New Jersey.

Residential

Clippership Wharf, East Boston, MA
A 370-unit housing development, situated on two piers in Boston Harbor, offering luxury, market rate and affordable housing.

The Park, Brookline, MA
The award-winning renovation of an abandoned hospital complex into 71 rental units in five restored buildings, and 16 condominium units in a new building on the site.

The Pavilion at Park Square, Boston, MA
An elegantly-designed, 350,000 square foot complex which houses ground floor retail space, five levels of offices and 100 condominium units.

Wellesley Continuing Care Retirement Community, Wellesley, MA
A 250-unit elderly housing complex, situated on 40 acres of land, which includes congregate housing, a 40-bed nursing home and a medical facility.

Urban Design

Commonwealth Flats, Boston, MA
Winner of an urban design competition for Phase Two of Boston's World Trade Center, this project consists of 1.7 million square feet of mixed-use space.

Olympic West Design Competition, Los Angeles, CA
Winner of an international design competition for a 20-block masterplan along Olympic Boulevard which includes two major high-rise office towers.

DESIGN PHILOSOPHY

Under the leadership of four principals, CBT's staff of architects, landscape architects, urban designers and interior architects operates in a team approach, taking advantage of a depth of experience and diversity of skills. Our projects, while varied in nature, are united by a commitment to design excellence and by a dedication to serving the individual needs of our clients with sensitivity and the highest degree of professional skill. CBT has established a national clientele and has been honored with more than sixty awards for design excellence.

We believe that good design grows out of many factors, but none is more fundamental than effective communication with our clients. We encourage a process of teamwork and involve clients in work sessions in a spirit of open exchange. This involvement promotes a precise understanding of the project and builds the mutual confidence so vital to a good solution. Today, the design process extends beyond the traditional boundaries of architect and client. Because design has become a process of negotiation between community interest groups, and public and regulatory agencies, communication and teamwork are critical to the success of each project.

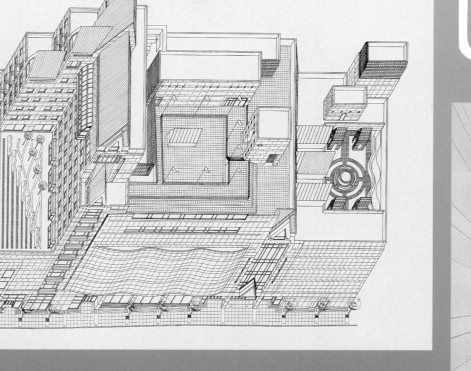

1. Otaru Crystal Court, Japan
   (Rendering)
2. Otaru Crystal Court, Japan
   (Isometric Rendition)
3. Matsuya Ginza, Japan
   (Model of interior escalator well)

CHAIX & JOHNSON INTERNATIONAL, INC.

ESTABLISHED DATE
Chaix & Johnson Architects - 1948
Chaix & Johnson Associates - 1961
Chaix & Johnson
International, Inc. - 1983

ADDRESSES

Corporate Headquarters
7060 Hollywood Boulevard
Los Angeles, CA 90028
Telephone (213) 461 3761
Facsimile (213) 467 4384
Telex   691503 CHAIJON LSA

Branch Offices
Chaix & Johnson International
(London)
28120 Hanway Street
London WIP 9DD, England
Telephone 637 1727
Facsimile   631 1120
Telex   297944 CNJLONG
Chaix & Johnson Designers
24 Peck Sean Street, Unit 02-10
Nehsons Building
Singapore 0207
Telephone   225 4288
Facsimile   225 9006
Telex   22908 CNJSIN

DIRECTORS
Wayne Y. Takeuchi, I.D.S.A., I.S.P.
- President, C.E.O.
Scott J. Kohno
- Executive V.P.
Edward H. Marquez
- Executive V.P.

NUMBER OF EMPLOYEES
51

PROJECT TYPES
Banks
Churches
Commercial
Government
Learning Institutions
Retail
Tourism/Leisure

DISCIPLINES
Architectural Design
Color & Materials
Construction
Graphics/Signage
Interior Design
Master Planning
Material Procurement
Planning/Merchandising
Production
Visual Presentation

PERSON TO CONTACT
Wayne Y. Takeuchi
Edward H. Marquez

CURRENT AND RECENT PROJECTS
(1987 TO PRESENT)

Commercial/Retail
East End Market, Adelaide, Australia 1988
El Puerto De Liverpool, Mexico City,
Mexico 1986/87
U. Yamane, Ltd., Honolulu, Hawaii 1989
Pacific Rim Leisure, Cairns, Australia 1989
Melbourne Central, Melbourne,
Australia 1988

Government
Changi PTB II Airport, Singapore 1989
Army Airforce Exchange Service, Dallas,
Texas 1987

Retail
Central Department Stores, Bangkok,
Thailand 1987
Bullock's Los Angeles, California 1988
Robinson's, Los Angeles, California 1987
Macy's, Sacramento, California 1988
Broadway, Los Angeles, California 1988
Allders International, Vancouver,
Canada 1987/88
Marui Imai, Sapporo, Japan 1987/89
Au Bon March, Paris, France 1988
Grandalia, Chihuahua, Mexico 1987
Daimaru, Inc., Osaka, Japan 1986/91
Matsuya, Tokyo, Japan 1986/90
Coppel, Mexicali, Mexico
Fabricas De Francia, Guadalajara,
Mexico 1987

Retail/Tourism Leisure
Marui Imai, Otaru, Japan 1988

PRIZES & AWARDS

Recent

1985
Honorable Mention for full line department
store remodel as established by National
Retailers Merchandising Association/
Institute of Store Planners.

> Marui Imai - Sapporo, Japan
> (Best Store Design - Japan)

1988
First Place Award for Supermarkets,
Specialty Food Retailing, Food Courts,
Convenience Stores by the National
Retailers Merchandising Association/
Institute of Store Planners.

> Marui Imai - Food Floors
> Sapporo, Japan

DESIGN PHILOSOPHY
Chaix & Johnson International is a group of
realistically imaginative people with a
common goal - that of successfully
addressing the challenges presented to us
by our clients. In our busy world of
individualism, a single element of most
importance stands out - "Image". Image is a
feeling, a reputation, and a message you
project. But Image doesn't just happen - it
must be promoted - visually - and must be
consistently supportive of the functional and
marketing goals of an organization.

Simply creating a beautiful building has
never been considered an adequate goal at
CJI. That building must serve our client's
functional business needs, project their
desired image and enhance their interests -
present and future. We feel that our designs
should transcend time. By creative
imagination, innovative design solutions and
implementing them effectively we would be
able to achieve timeless architecture. One
of the secrets of our success is the ability to
integrate skilful client-designer
communication. Our clients are actually
involved in all phases of their project, and
the integral role they play contributes
greatly to the ultimate success of their
projects.

The strength and stability of the firm is
evidenced by the volume of "repeat"
business from well satisfied clients over a
period of 40 years.

HISTORY AND PRACTICE
Chaix & Johnson International was founded
in 1948 by Alfred V. Chaix and R. Walter
Johnson. Known as C & J Architects, at the
time, the focus of their work was storefronts,
drive-ins and churches in the Southern
California area. In 1948 Chaix & Johnson
started their work for the Broadway
Department Store which began Chaix &
Johnson's entrance into retail work, an area
the company is renowned for. Chaix &
Johnson International's valued reputation as
experts in the field of retail store and
shopping center design have attracted
clientele located throughout the world with
its international assignments beginning in
1968 with Isetan Department stores of
Tokyo, Japan. Chaix & Johnson later
opened two branch offices - one in Singapore
and one in London - to better service
international projects.

Perhaps lesser known, but equally
exceptional, are the designs we have created
in other sectors, including churches,
learning institutions, and banks. Regardless
of the type and scope of a project, we bring
the same dedication and enthusiasm to each
assignment starting where we know it is
essential to begin - with the right image.

CLARK HOLMAN & MOORHEAD, LTD.

P. Clark   I. Holman   R. Moorhead

CLARK HOLMAN & MOORHEAD, LTD.
Architects & Engineers

CHRONOLOGY OF PRACTICE
Elken & Clark - 1958

Clark, Elken & Holman - 1959-1963

Clark & Holman - 1963-1976

Clark Holman & Moorhead, Ltd. - 1976 to Present

ADDRESS
808 Second Avenue North
Fargo, ND 58102

TELEPHONE
(701) 237 6836

FACSIMILE
(701) 237 3455

DIRECTORS
Perry S. Clark,
AIA, B. Arch (Hons), NCARB
Irvin C. Holman,
AIA, PE, B.S. AE, NCARB
Richard A. Moorhead,
AIA, B. Arch. (Hons), NCARB

NUMBER OF EMPLOYEES
6 Registered Architects
1 Structural Engineer
1 Undergraduate
1 Administrative Assistant/
  Secretary

PROJECT TYPES
Health Care	40%
Office and Commercial	30%
Educational	20%
Residential	5%
Other	5%

LICENSED TO PRACTICE
North Dakota
South Dakota
Minnesota
Wisconsin
Florida
NCARB

HONORS AND AWARDS
16 AIA Merit and Honor Awards

CURRENT VALUE OF WORK IN PROGRESS
$7 million

CURRENT AND RECENT PROJECTS
Veterans Administration Medical Center,
Addition for Clinical Improvements,
Fargo, ND.
6 levels, Construction Cost $14m.

Cass County Courthouse,
Restoration and North and South Wings,
Fargo, ND.
6 levels, Construction Cost $4.5m.

Student Dormitory,
North Dakota State University,
Fargo, ND.
10 levels, Construction Cost $4m.

Out-patient Facility,
Dakota Medical Center,
Fargo, ND.
4 levels, Construction Cost $2.6m.

Vertical Expansion,
Dakota Clinic,
Fargo, ND.
8 levels, Construction Cost $3.6m.

Additions and Alterations,
Forum Publishing Company,
Fargo, ND.
5 levels, Construction Cost $2.7m.

North Wing Additions,
Dakota Clinic,
Fargo, ND.
3 levels, Construction Cost $6.2m.

Health Center Addition,
Pelican Rapids, MN.
1 level, Construction Cost $0.3m.

School Additions,
Hawley, MN.
1 level, Construction Cost $1m.

Northern Crops Institute,
North Dakota State University,
Fargo, ND.
3 levels, Construction Cost $1.5m.

Church Addition,
Hope Lutheran Church,
Fargo, ND.
2 levels, Construction Cost $1m.

Parking Ramp,
Dakota Medical Center,
Fargo, ND.
(284 cars - foundations for 8 levels)
3 levels, Construction Cost $1.4m.

FIRM PHILOSOPHY
Clark Holman & Moorhead, Ltd. is a small firm with a highly professional staff: six registered architects, one structural engineer, one undergraduate student and secretarial staff. All principals and staff become personally involved in each project.

We have been asked if we 'specialize' in any building type. Our specialty is Architecture, the basic philosophy and tools for which apply to any building type. Our practice encompasses commissions from residential kitchens and porches to multi-million dollar, highly technical hospital projects with a design integrity devoid of transitory design cliches. Architectural form is drawn from the functional need for which the building exists, from the physical locations, whether natural or man made and from influences of the community.

An important characteristic of our practice is the caliber of working relationships that have been formed with firms that offer a wide range of professional expertise. It is our policy to retain the consultants that we deem most qualified for each specific project.

The aim of our firm is to bring physical comfort and visual joy and pleasure to those who habitate our structures.

COOPER CARRY & ASSOCIATES, INC.

**COOPER CARRY &
ASSOCIATES, INC.**

ESTABLISHED DATE
1960

ADDRESSES
3520 Piedmont Road
Suite 200
Atlanta, GA 30305-1595
Telephone   (404) 237 2000
Facsimile   (404) 237 0276

1133 Connecticut Avenue, N.W.
Washington, DC 20036-4302
Telephone   (202) 785 4800

DIRECTORS
Jerome M. Cooper, FAIA
Walter T. Carry, FAIA
Kevin R. Cantley, AIA
Joyce P. McCullough
Sanford M. Nelson, AIA
E. Pope Bullock, AIA
Ted S. Gum, AIA
Richard S. Hall, AIA
Helen Davis Hatch, AIA
Ara Keyfer, AIA

NUMBER OF EMPLOYEES
175

SERVICES RENDERED
Master Planning
Architecture
Landscape Architecture
Interior Architecture

PROJECT TYPES
Corporate Office Buildings
Investment Office Buildings
Hotels
Resorts
Retail Malls
Specialty Retail Centers
Mixed-Use Developments

PERSON TO CONTACT
Atlanta, GA
Jerome M. Cooper, FAIA
Telephone (404) 237 2000

Washington, DC
Sanford M. Nelson, AIA
Telephone (202) 785 4800

University of Chicago, Law Library

Beaver Valley National Zoological Park

D.C. Center for Therapeutic Recreation

Southland Corp. Regional Headquarters

Dominican House of Studies,
Theological Library

Southland Corporation Regional Headquarters

Vietnam Veteran's Memorial

COOPER • LECKY

**COOPER • LECKY,
ARCHITECTS, P.C.**
Architecture
Planning
Interiors

ESTABLISHED
1963

ADDRESS
1000 Potomac Street, N.W.
Washington, DC 20007

TELEPHONE
(202) 333 2310

FACSIMILE
(202) 333 6962

PRINCIPALS
W. Kent Cooper, AIA
William Lecky, AIA
Roger Burns
Robert Sangine, AIA

ASSOCIATES
Jeanne Adams, IBD
Carol Moore Brust, AIA
May Wood Carr, AIA
Charles Clements
James Cummings
Michael T. Foster, AIA
Joann Satullo Manzek, ASID
Barry Weiner, AIA

STAFF SIZE
40

PERSON TO CONTACT
W. Kent Cooper

PROFILE

Cooper • Lecky of Washington, DC offers architecture, planning and interior design. Established in 1963 by W. Kent Cooper, Associate of the late Eero Saarinen and Architectural Project Manager for the development of Dulles International Airport, the firm has grown to forty persons.

Early years brought the firm transportation, education and religious facilities and an architectural consultancy for the US Department of Commerce, Office of International Expositions, which led to an active role in the design of the US Pavilions for Expo's '82 and '84.

Cooper • Lecky's involvement with exhibitory for World Fairs was enhanced with an ongoing relationship with the Smithsonian's National Zoological Park. Projects include a zoo master plan, the "Beaver Valley" aquatic mammal exhibit, and the Gibbon exhibit. "Amazonia", currently on the boards, is an aquatic tropical rainforest exhibit that replicates a section of the Amazon River complete with animals, vegetation, and rain.

A natural extension of the firm's zoo designs, animal research and bio-medical facilities are an important aspect of the practice. Laboratories for the National Institutes of Health and a variety of public and private research facilities have been designed at all levels of bio-hazard containment.

Many of Cooper • Lecky's projects have been prototypical and have required extensive investigation to produce a "state of the art" building. An example of this would be the nationally recognized DC Center for Therapeutic Recreation. It is the first complex in the country that focused on the special needs of retarded and handicapped youth and adults. This project was instrumental in the development of current barrier-free design standards.

Cooper • Lecky's strength in libraries is clearly demonstrated in the addition/renovation of The University of Chicago's Law Library. In 1956 Cooper served as Saarinen's Project Architect on the original structure and was well suited to interpret the original Saarinen design intent.

A master plan was drawn to organize and restore the integrity of monastic life to the Dominican House of Studies (circa 1905) in Washington, DC. A new academic complex complete with auditorium, classrooms and 100,000 volume library was planned and the original Priory was restored to its intended cloistered environment.

The Interior Design Department has planned over five million square feet of space in the last five years. Major projects include the headquarters for the Strategic Defense Initiative Organization, The White House Press Room, the International Trade Commision's central offices and the Southland Corporation Regional Headquarters.

The firm received a Presidential Design Award as well as the Henry Bacon Medal for memorial architecture for their work as Architect of Record on the Vietnam Veteran's Memorial. Designed, in conjunction with Maya Lin, the memorial is one of the most visited monuments in Washington.

Interest in passive solar design and natural daylighting have also led to numerous design awards from the American Institute of Architects.

Cooper • Lecky strives to maintain a diverse balance of work. In-house specialty teams exist for Historic Preservation, Exhibition, Interiors, Lab/R&D, Daycare, Recreation, Food Service, Education and Library and Performing Arts Facilities.

Cooper • Lecky Architects views its work as a service, not as an end in itself. Success is evaluated on how well each design supports the needs and aspirations of each client.

PROJECTS & AWARDS

United States Pavilion Theaters, Expo '84, New Orleans, LA

Beaver Valley, National Zoological Park, Washington, DC

Astronomy Laboratory, US Naval Observatory, Washington, DC

Smithsonian Environmental Research Center, Edgewater, MD

DC Center for Therapeutic Recreation, Washington, DC,
AIA Award for Design Excellence

The University of Chicago, Law Library, Chicago, IL

Dominican House of Studies, Academic Complex, Washington, DC

Fort Meade, Youth Activities & Recreation Center, Fort Meade, MD

Pohick Church Parish House,
AIA Award for Historic Preservation

Southland Corporation Regional Headquarters, Alexandria, VA

Strategic Defense Initiative Organization, The Pentagon, Washington, DC

Vietnam Veteran's Memorial, Washington, DC, Henry Bacon Medal,
AIA Design Honor Award,
Presidential Design Award

1. Westin Hotel at the San Francisco International Airport
   Photography by: Russell Abraham
2. Harbor Court Hotel, Baltimore, MD
   Photography by: Gregory Murphey
3. Peat Marwick Main & Co. Offices, Washington, DC
   Photography by: Gregory Murphey
4. Creighton University Student Center, Omaha, NE
   Photography by: P. Drickey

LEO A DALY

Leo A. Daly

LEO A DALY
Planning • Architecture •
Engineering • Interiors

ESTABLISHED DATE
1915

ADDRESSES

Headquarters
8600 Indian Hills Drive
Omaha, NE 68114
Telephone (402) 391 8111
Facsimile   (402) 391 8564

Other Offices
Hong Kong
- Leo A. Daly Pacific Ltd.
Singapore - Leo A. Daly Design
Consultants PTE. Ltd
Tokyo - Nihon-Daly
Riyadh, Saudi Arabia
Madrid - Daly-Law Iberica, S.A.
Honolulu, HI
Los Angeles, CA
San Francisco, CA
Phoenix, AZ
Seattle, WA
St. Louis, MO
Washington, DC
Chantilly, VA (Dulles Int'l. Airport)
Atlanta, GA

DIRECTORS
Leo A. Daly, AIA, RIBA, ARIA
John M. Free, AIA, RIBA, PE
Ronald K. Leiferman
Fred J. Matthies, PE, FICE
Edward F. Cambridge, PE
Joseph D. Vaccaro, AIA
James M. Ingram, AIA
John C. Broderick, AIA, PE

NUMBER OF EMPLOYEES
709

PERSON TO CONTACT
Fred J. Matthies - Senior Vice President

PROJECT TYPES

Commercial
Office Buildings
Hotels/Resorts
Condominiums/Apartments
Retail Stores/Shopping Centers
Restaurants/Clubs

Computer/Command/Control/ Communications
Computer/Data Centers
Technical Operations Centers
Telephone/Television/Radio Stations
Secured/Hardened Facilities

Science and Industry
Research Centers/Laboratories
Distribution Centers/Warehouses
Assembly/Processing Plants

Transportation
Airport Terminals
Gate Position Studies
Control Towers/Base Buildings
Wharfs/Piers/Docks
Highways/Bridges/Parking Facilities

PROJECT TYPES
Institutional
Educational
Health care
Civic
Postal
Criminal Justice
Recreational
Life Care Communities

OTHER DISCIPLINES
Planning
Civil Engineering
Structural Engineering
Mechanical Engineering
Electrical Engineering
Interior Design Services
Computer Aided Design
Transportation Engineering
Urban Design
Program Management
Facilities Management

CURRENT OR RECENT PROJECTS
District Center Redevelopment,
Frankston, Australia
- in association with Tompkins
Shaw & Evans Pty. Ltd.
Shearson Lehman
- American Express Offices, Hong Kong
Motorola "Silicon Harbour" Plant,
Hong Kong
IBM Offices, Hong Kong
HONVEST Tower, Honolulu, HI
Ilikai Hotel Renovation, Honolulu, HI
- in association with Nihon Architects,
Engineers and Consultants, Inc.
Terminal No. 2, Los Angeles
International Airport, Los Angeles, CA
Westin Hotel, San Francisco
International Airport, San Francisco, CA
ConAgra Corporate Headquarters,
Omaha, NE
Harbor Court Mixed-Use Complex,
Baltimore, MD

DESIGN PHILOSOPHY/HISTORY
Leo A. Daly is an international firm offering
professional design services in the fields of
architecture, planning, engineering and
interiors. Our company consists of nearly
700 professional staff members -- graduates
of more than 100 colleges and universities.

In establishing his practice in 1915, Leo A.
Daly, Sr., set exacting standards for design
excellence. Defense-related projects for the
U.S. Armed Forces initiated major firm
growth under the direction of Leo A. Daly,
Jr. which continued in the 1960s and 1970s
in the fields of education, health care and
research.

Today, Leo A. Daly, AIA, RIBA, ARIA continues
the high standards of design excellence set
by his father and grandfather. Since his
appointment as President, he has extended
the firm's commitment to global promotion
of design excellence with the creation of
international business associations. These
include the formation of Nihon-Daly, an
association with a Tokyo-based international
architectural, engineering and consulting
firm, to serve multinational clients; an
association with Saudi Consulting House, an
agency of the Saudi Arabian Government;
and an agreement to associate with the
China State Construction Engineering
Corporation (CSCEC) for projects in the
Republic of China. Most recently, Daly has
formed a joint company with widely
recognized geoscience consultants, Law
Engineering, to pursue opportunities with
Mediterranean Area clients.

DPK&A

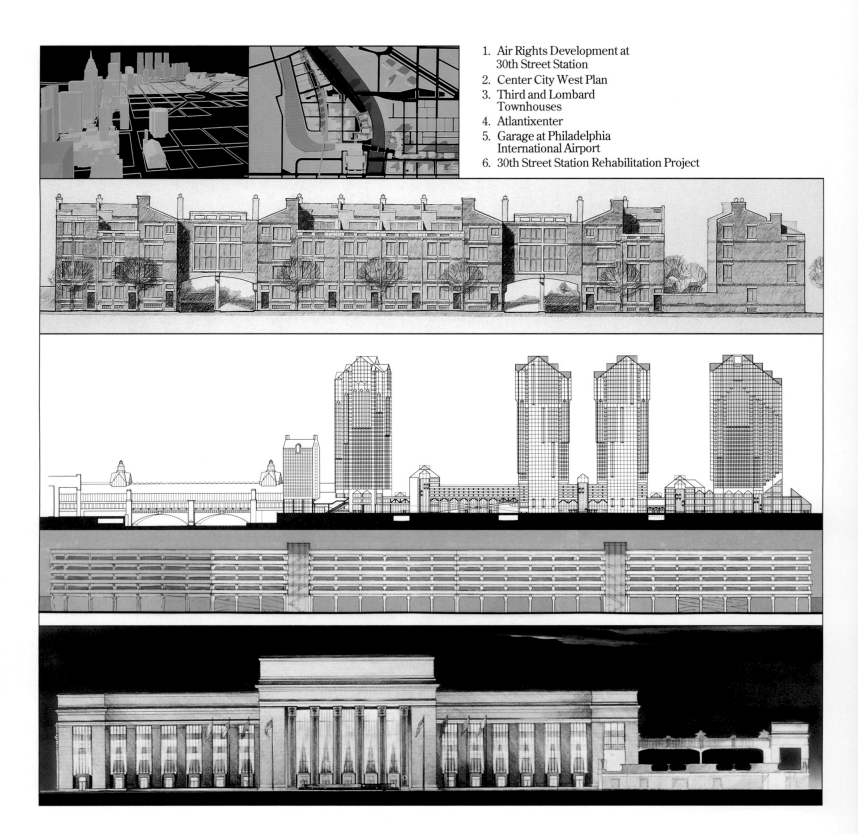

1. Air Rights Development at 30th Street Station
2. Center City West Plan
3. Third and Lombard Townhouses
4. Atlantixenter
5. Garage at Philadelphia International Airport
6. 30th Street Station Rehabilitation Project

DAN PETER KOPPLE & ASSOCIATES

DAN PETER KOPPLE & ASSOCIATES
Architecture • Urban Design
• Planning

ESTABLISHED DATE
1976

ADDRESS
1611 Walnut Street
Philadelphia, PA 19103

TELEPHONE
(215) 568 7350

FACSIMILE
(215) 568 0785

PRINCIPAL
Dan Peter Kopple, AIA

NUMBER OF EMPLOYEES
15

PROJECT TYPES
Aviation Facilities
Interiors & Space Planning
Medical Facilities
Mixed-Use Air Rights
Parking Structures
Planning
Residential Development
Transportation/Restoration

OTHER DISCIPLINES
CAD Applications

PERSON TO CONTACT
Dan Peter Kopple, AIA

CURRENT AND RECENT PROJECTS

Aviation Facilities
Roadway Study, International Airport,
for Phila. Dept. of Commerce
Concession Development Program,
International Airport, for Phila. Dept. of
Commerce
Garage A-B, International Airport,
for Phila. Parking Authority
Maintenance Building, International Airport,
for Phila. Dept. of Commerce

Interiors & Space Planning
Real Estate Development Office,
Philadelphia, PA , for Amerimar Realty Co.
Insurance Office, Philadelphia, PA,
for Bayly, Martin & Fay, Inc.
Railroad Office, Philadelphia, PA, for Amtrak

Medical Facilities
Medical Building, Philadelphia, PA,
for SPMG
Doctors' Offices, Carlisle, PA,
for Reconstructive Surgery

Mixed-Use Air Rights Development
Amtrak Rail Yards, Philadelphia, PA,
for Gerald D. Hines Interests
Atlantixenter, Philadelphia, PA,
for Atlantixenter Properties
Penn Center West, Philadelphia, PA,
for Penn Center West Associates

Parking Structures
Garage A-B, International Airport,
for Phila. Parking Authority
Performing Arts, Philadelphia, PA, for PICPA
Short-Term, 30th Street Station, for Amtrak

Planning
Center City West, Philadelphia, PA,
for Maguire Thomas, PECO, Amtrak,
Atlantixenter, Gerald D. Hines Interests
Air Rights, 30th Street Station,
for Gerald D. Hines Interests

Residential Development
Third & Lombard, Philadelphia, PA, for TDG
Gravers Lane, Chestnut Hill, PA, private

Transportation/Restoration
30th St. Station, Philadelphia, PA, for Amtrak
Commuter Station, Westfield, NJ,
for NJ Transit

DESIGN PHILOSOPHY/HISTORY
Dan Peter Kopple & Associates is
committed to architectural, urban design
and planning pursuits. Our practice meets
changes in society and technology with
inventive approaches and state-of-the-art
architectural solutions which honor and
preserve traditional architectural excellence.

DPK&A's emphasis is on development
projects requiring the integration of multiple
programs. Our expertise in the leadership
of many specialized consultants provides the
unity vital to a well-integrated, functional
and attractive product.

Dan Peter Kopple and Associates began in
1976 as Dan Peter Kopple, AIA,
subsequently to become Kopple, Sheward &
Day in 1977. Projects under the auspices of
this firm ranged in scope from restoration of
historic buildings to planning for large scale
development as well as on-going work at the
Philadelphia International Airport. In 1984,
Dan Peter Kopple and Associates was
formed and continues serving both public
agencies and private clients.

We are enthusiastic about our work. We
have the people, experience and tools to
serve our clients well. We use care,
understanding and imagination to guide our
clients to successful solutions.

1

2

3

4

DELAWIE
BRETTON
WILKES

ASSOCIATES AIA

ARCHITECTURE
PLANNING

5

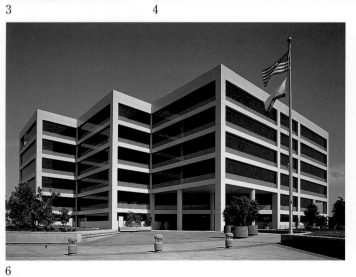

6

7

8   9

1. Gateway Medical Offices, San Diego
2. Mission Valley Regional Shopping Center, San Diego
3. Giraffe Exhibit, San Diego Zoo, San Diego
4. Metropolitan Transit System Headquarters, San Diego
5. Shark Encounter, Sea World, Orlando
6. Police Administration Center, San Diego
7. Old Ferry Landing Retail Complex, San Diego
8. Residence Halls, University of California, at San Diego, La Jolla
9. Plaza de Balboa, San Diego

DELAWIE/BRETTON/WILKES ASSOCIATES

Directors (L-R): M. Rodrigues, J. Barker,
M. Wilkes, J. Bretton and H. Delawie

DELAWIE/BRETTON/WILKES ASSOCIATES
Architecture and Planning

ESTABLISHED DATE
1961

ADDRESS
2827 Presidio Drive
San Diego, CA 92110

TELEPHONE
(619) 299 6690

FACSIMILE
(619) 299 5513

DIRECTORS
Homer Delawie, FAIA
- Chairman of the Board
Michael B. Wilkes, AIA - President
James Barker, AIA - Vice President
John Bretton, CSI - Vice President
M. Andrew Rodrigues, AIA
- Vice President

NUMBER OF EMPLOYEES
22

PROJECT TYPES
Aquariums and Zoos
Educational Facilities
Government Facilities
Master Planning
Medical Office Facilities
Mid/High Rise Office Buildings
Military Housing/Training
Buildings
Recreation Projects
Regional/Specialty Retail

OTHER DISCIPLINES
Interior Design
Landscape Architecture
Master Planning
Programming
Space Planning

PERSON TO CONTACT
Homer Delawie, FAIA
Michael B. Wilkes, AIA

CURRENT AND RECENT PROJECTS

Aquariums and Zoos
Shark Exhibits, Sea World,
San Diego, Orlando
Penguin Encounters, Sea World,
San Diego, Cleveland
Lake Superior Center, Duluth, MN
Children's Zoo, San Diego Zoo, San Diego
Great Ape, Ungulate, Reptile, Elephant
Exhibits, San Diego Zoo, San Diego

Educational Facilities
UCSD Third College Residence Hall and
Student Center, San Diego
School for the Creative and Performing Arts,
San Diego
SDSU Life Science Classroom and Office
Building, San Diego
San Diego Police Academy, San Diego

Government Facilities
Metropolitan Transit Headquarters
(High Rise), San Diego
Police Administration and Technical Center,
San Diego
Coronado Library, Coronado

Master Planning
Naval Electronics Center, San Diego
First San Diego River Improvement Plan,
San Diego
Old Town San Diego Master Plan,
San Diego
Water Oriented Recreation Facility, Naval
Amphibious Base, San Diego

Medical Facilities
Ambulatory Care Building at UCSD Satellite
Medical Center, San Diego
San Diego Hospice Center, San Diego
Headquarters Area Dispensary, Camp
Pendleton Marine Corp Base

Mid/High Rise Office
Silvergate Congregate Living Tower (High
Rise), San Diego
Gateway Medical Office Building, San Diego
Guest Quarters Hotel/Starboard Station
(High Rise), San Diego
Tyson Plaza (High Rise), San Diego

Military Housing/Training Buildings
Submarine Training Facility Building,
San Diego
Fleet Anti-Submarine Training Building,
San Diego
Unaccompanied Enlisted Personnel
Housing, Fort Irwin

Recreational Projects
Lawrence Jewish Community Center,
San Diego
Linda Vista Gymnasium, San Diego

Regional/Specialty Retail
Mission Valley Regional Center
Expansion/Renovation, San Diego
The Old Ferry Landing, San Diego
Loma Village, San Diego
Fashion Valley Center Retail Expansion,
San Diego

PROFILE
Delawie/Bretton/Wilkes Associates, a
San Diego based firm, is recognized for
design excellence in architecture and
planning with expertise in aquarium design
and zoological projects.

Established in 1961, the corporation is led
by founding partner, Homer Delawie FAIA.
A team approach to design has resulted in
the receipt of over 45 design awards for
works completed and in progress both
nationally and internationally. In 1986, the
firm received the San Diego Chapter
American Institute of Architects
Outstanding Firm Award for significant
contributions to architecture and the
community.

During its thirty year history, DBWA has
experienced a diversity of clients and
projects ranging from single family
residences to high rise commercial office
buildings. Commissions include designs for
federal, state, and local agencies as well as
buildings in the corporate and private
sectors.

DBWA's full range of architectural and
planning services are continually upgraded
and enhanced by sophisticated
communications and computer systems to
anticipate future technological needs in
design and production.

Currently the partners hold licenses in
Arizona, California, Florida, Minnesota,
Ohio, and Texas. In addition members of
the firm hold NCARB certificates and are
licensed in England, Denmark, and Canada.

PHILOSOPHY
The hallmark of DBWA's success is a
commitment to excellence achieved
through the partners' active participation on
every project from inception to completion.
This ensures the highest quality of design
and project coordination and also provides
attention to detail at all phases of project
development by the firm's highly skilled
leadership. The triumph of this philosophy
is reflected by award recognition,
competition winning designs, and long
standing clientele.

The professional staff with resources in
interior design and landscape architecture
can be expanded to include the resources of
consultants to meet the complexities of
special commissions.

DEMAREST & ASSOCIATES ARCHITECTS, INC.

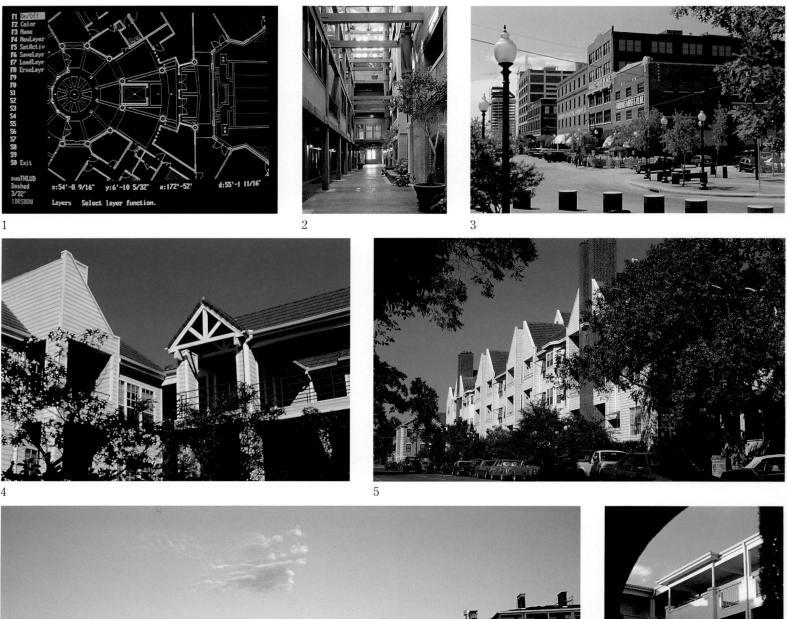

1

2

3

4

5

6

7

1. The Island on Lake Travis, Lago Vista, TX
2. Market-Ross Place, Dallas, TX
3. Market-Ross Place, Dallas, TX
4. Centennial Condominiums, Austin, TX
5. Centennial Condominiums, Austin, TX
6. The Island on Lake Travis, Lago Vista, TX
7. The Island on Lake Travis, Lago Vista, TX

D. Demarest   R. Lamkin

DEMAREST & ASSOCIATES ARCHITECTS, INC.

ESTABLISHED
1982

ADDRESS
703 McKinney Avenue
Suite 400
Dallas, TX 75202

TELEPHONE
(214) 720 0188

FACSIMILE
(214) 880 7526

PRINCIPAL
David T. Demarest, AIA

ASSOCIATE
Robert W. Lamkin, AIA

PROJECT TYPES
Commercial
Computer Aided Design
  Services
Facility Management
Renovation/Restoration
Residential
  Multi-family
  - Retirement Communities
  - Student Oriented
    Communities
  - Loft Residences/Studios
  - Garden Apartments
  - Townhouses
  Single Family Homes
Restaurants and Prototypes
Retail Design
Space Planning

PERSON TO CONTACT
David T. Demarest

CURRENT AND RECENT PROJECTS

Resort/retirement community
The Island on Lake Travis

Adaptive reuse office/retail/restaurant
Market-Ross Place
The Brewery
The West End Marketplace
West End Brewing Company

Student Oriented Housing
University of Georgia
University of Arkansas
Auburn University
Mississippi State University
University of Texas
Virginia Polytechnical Institute

General Office/Space Planning
Dallas Area Rapid Transit
Otis Engineering

Office
Midway Place
Forest Tower

COMPANY PROFILE

Demarest & Associates Architects, Inc. has grown in size and reputation since their founding in 1982, becoming known for outstanding high-density multi-family design, as well as successful commercial building design, restaurants, award winning historic renovation projects, and computer applications in architecture. The firm's offices are located in a renovated warehouse building on the edge of downtown Dallas' West End Historic District.

Demarest & Associates Architects, Inc. is a personal service oriented company that strives to fulfill the expectation of their clients through quality design, building technology, and budget considerations. Projects have been innovative, well conceived, and profitable for all parties. The firm emphasizes qualified, personal service by its Principal and Associates.

Computer technology has revolutionized the traditional architectural office. Computer assisted design & drafting allows the firm to respond more quickly and with increased flexibility to the clients' needs. A fully integrated 2D/3D data-based CADD system allows for a more complete service, aiding our clients in marketing, facilities management, desk top publishing, and construction take-offs.

David Demarest is a member of the American Institute of Architects and certified by the National Council of Architectural Registration Boards. He is a member of the Construction Specifications Institute, the International Conference of Building Officials, and the Historic Preservation League.

THE OAHU BAR

DESIGN PARTNERS INCORPORATED

Principals (L-R): O. Chock, V. Inoshita,
J. Aveiro and M. Goshi

DESIGN PARTNERS INCORPORATED

ESTABLISHED
1979

ADDRESS
1251 South King Street, Suite D
Honolulu, HI 96813

TELEPHONE
(808) 531 0102

TELECOPIER
(808) 533 6942

PARTNERS
Owen Chock, AIA CSI
Vernon Inoshita, AIA
John Aveiro, AIA
Michael Goshi, AIA

STAFF
22

PROJECT TYPES
Housing
- Affordable
- Market
- Senior
Institutional
- Government Offices
- Churches
- Schools
- Auditorium/Food Facilities
Commercial
- Shopping Centers
- Shops/Stores
- Offices
- Restaurants
Industrial
- Special Military Facilities
- Warehouses
- Automotive Shops
Recreational
- Multipurpose Buildings
- Arts & Crafts/Exhibition Rooms
- Gymnasium/Sports Facilities
- Golf Clubhouse/Amphitheatre
Medical-Dental/Medical Offices
- Health Clinics
Hotels/Apartments
Building Restoration

ORGANIZATIONS
American Institute of Architects
Construction Specifications Institute

SERVICES
Architecture
Interior Architecture
Graphic Design
Space Planning
Land Planning
Feasibility Studies
Computer Support Services

REPRESENTATIVE PROJECTS

Housing
The La'ilani (Kona)
Mililani New Town (Oahu)
Colony Ridge (Makakilo)
Waikoloa Shores (Hawaii)

Institutional
Honolulu City Hall Additions
Trinity Missionary Church (Pearl Harbor)
Credit Union Building (Hickam)
Hawaii Baptist Academy (Honolulu)

Commercial
Thomas Square Center Condominium
Offices (Honolulu)
The Oahu Bar - Sheraton Waikiki
KAIM Radio Station/Transmitter Building
(Molokai)
Office Building for King Birch Development
(Honolulu)
Bowling Alley for Central Pacific
Development (Nanakuli)

Industrial
Various Military Projects
(Pearl Harbor, Hickam, Kaneohe)
Maintenance Facilities for the City and
County of Honolulu
Hygrade Electric Facilities (Oahu)

Recreational
Ala Wai Golf Clubhouse (Honolulu)
Mililani Arts & Crafts Center
Kalakaua Recreation Center (Honolulu)
Mauna Lani Golf Course Buildings (Hawaii)
Waikiki Shell Amphitheater Addition

Medical - Dental Offices
Wahiawa Medical Offices
Various Offices in Honolulu

Hotels/Apartments
Pacific Beach Hotel (Waikiki)
Sheraton Waikiki - Interior (Waikiki)
Hale Koa Hotel - Revisions (Waikiki)
Kuhio Village Hotel (Waikiki)
Hawaii Monarch Hotel Restaurant (Waikiki)

Building Restoration
Haili Church (Hilo)
The Armstrong Building (Honolulu)
One North Hotel Building (Honolulu)

PROFILE
Design Partners Incorporated (DPI) was
founded in 1979 and is committed to
providing a high degree of individualized
principal involvement in all projects from
concept to construction. Eight of the present
twenty two person staff are registered
architects, providing professional care in
design, production, client communication
and project management.

Prior to the formation of Design Partners,
the principals had contributed to such
projects as the World Trade Center in New
York, the Century Building in Los Angeles,
the Honolulu International Airport, and
major hotels in Hawaii and the Pacific area.
Since the formation of the firm, the
principals have been privileged to design an
impressive cross section of Hawaii's
architectural scene.

Communication and servicing
responsibilities are done by the designated
partner in charge coupled with a project
architect/designer for each assignment.
This modified team concept involves a cadre
of support from the rest of the staff in
response to the magnitude of the work
scope. This has enabled the office to handle
several large projects simultaneously. DPI
has also integrated an extensive use of
computer aided design techniques as a
further commitment to effective project
processing.

Because of Hawaii's burgeoning need for
housing at all levels, DPI has developed an
especial expertise in this area, having done
an array of housing types in the several
levels of the residential market in Hawaii
ranging from affordable multi-family
housing to upscale single family residences.
Design Partners is currently serving as
design consultant to the two most
prestigious residential developments in
Honolulu. This expertise has resulted in a
number of awards for the firm in the
residential design area.

Because of the diversity of business and
resort activities found in the islands, Design
Partners has designed a variety of building
types such as offices, shops, restaurants and
other commercial projects. Coupled with
their housing background, their capabilities
in the institutional/recreational facilities
areas, and their experience in special
purpose buildings for the military, Design
Partners Incorporated is well positioned to
maintain its leading role in Hawaii and the
Pacific Rim building scene.

Valley Lutheran Hospital

Phoenix Sky Harbor International
Airport Terminal 3

Industrial Commission of Arizona

Sun Devil Stadium South Entrance Expansion

Phoenix Elks Lodge #335

DWL ARCHITECTS + PLANNERS, INC.

ESTABLISHED
1949

ADDRESS
2600 North Central Avenue
Suite 219
Phoenix, AZ 85004

TELEPHONE
(602) 264 9731

FACSIMILE
(602) 264 1928

DIRECTORS
Richard E. Drover, AIA
James Lindlan, AIA
Carle W. Van Deman, AIA
Lawrence E. Metcalf, AIA
Michael L. Haake, AIA

NUMBER OF EMPLOYEES
30

PROJECT TYPES

Community
Community Centers, Zoos

Educational
Libraries, Colleges and
Universities

Government
Commercial and General
Aviation Terminals, Military
Installations, Municipal
Buildings

Health Care
Acute Care, Long-Term Care,
Specialty Diagnostic/Treatment
Centers and Medical Office
Buildings

Industrial
Warehouse/Maintenance
Complex

OTHER DISCIPLINES
Facility Consulting
Interior Design
Master Planning

PERSON TO CONTACT
Lawrence E. Metcalf, AIA

Principals (L-R): C. Van Deman, J. Lindlan, L. Metcalf, M. Haake

CURRENT AND RECENT PROJECTS

Community
Phoenix Zoo, Exhibits and Support
Facilities, Phoenix, AZ
Phoenix Elk's Lodge #335, Phoenix, AZ

Educational
Noble Science & Engineering Library,
Arizona State University, Tempe, AZ
Music Building Addition, Arizona State
University. In association with
The Mathes Group
Sun Devil Stadium South Entrance
Expansion, Arizona State University,
Tempe, AZ

Government
Industrial Commission of Arizona, Six Story
Municipal Office Building, Phoenix, AZ
Phoenix Sky Harbor International Airport,
Passenger Terminals 3 & 4, Phoenix, AZ
Prescott Municipal Airport, General Aviation
Terminal, Prescott, AZ

Health Care
Community Hospital Medical Center,
Patient Wing Addition, New Obstetrics Unit
and New Architectural Finishes and
Furnishings for Entire Hospital, Phoenix, AZ
Doctor's Hospital Medical Center, Medical
Office Building, Colorado Springs, CO
Maryvale Samaritan Hospital, New 256 Bed
Acute Care Hospital and Outpatient Care
Center, Phoenix, AZ
Humana Hospital Mountainview, New 172
Bed Acute Care Facility and Medical Office
Building, Thornton, CO
South Coast Medical Center, Complete
Hospital Refurbishing including Master
Interior Color and Finish Schedule and New
Adolescent Psychiatric Unit,
South Laguna, CA
United States Coast Guard Support Center,
Medical and Dental Facility with Full
Trauma Capabilities, Kodiak, AK
Valley Lutheran Hospital, New 120 Bed
Acute Care Hospital, Mesa, AZ
Whittier Hospital Medical Center, New
Obstetrics Addition, Whittier, CA

HISTORY
What began as the fortuitous Partnership of
Weaver & Drover Architects in 1949 and
reorganized as Drover Welch & Lindlan
Architects in 1969, has developed into one of
the most sophisticated, energetic design
firms in the Southwest today ... DWL
Architects + Planners, Inc. As one of the
oldest architectural practices in Arizona, the
firm has maintained continuity, yet
progressive direction, throughout its forty
year evolution.

PROFILE
The group's success is driven by the firm's
unique management philosophy and
commitment to personal service. Each
project undertaken by the firm is under the
disciplined guidance and direction of a DWL
Principal who is accountable to the client.
By providing this professional attention and
consideration to the clients' specific needs,
the firm has gained an extremely loyal
clientele.

Headquartered in Phoenix, Arizona, the firm
is recognized throughout the Western
United States for solving complex problems.
This acceptance has allowed DWL to
expand its services on a regional basis from
the Aleutian chain in Alaska to the Gulf
Coast of Texas.

The depth of field and diversity of the firm's
professional services are augmented by a
staff of highly trained professionals using
sophisticated computer systems. The
combination of this expertise and
technological advancement has kept DWL
in the forefront of achievement.

DESIGN PHILOSOPHY
For over forty years, the firm has created
thought provoking buildings which are
innovative examples of the best in
architectural design. Viewing architecture
as a problem solving approach to the
fundamental issues of people, place and
purpose has allowed DWL to solve difficult
and unusual project challenges.

The firm's design ethic is a contemporary
expression of classical values derived from
thoughtful form and space manipulation.
This attention to detail in form and function
and the recognition of art in architecture
translates into innovative, cost efficient,
quality design, free from temporary and
trendy influences.

DWL Architects + Planners, Inc. ... a forty
year heritage of quality design and service.

1

2

1. Bradley International Terminal
2. Federal Reserve Bank/Los Angeles Branch
3. American Honda Research & Development
4. Federal Reserve Bank/Los Angeles Branch
5. Northrop Division Headquarters
6. The City Tower
7. Hewlett Packard Regional Office

3

5

6

7

DWORSKY ASSOCIATES, ARCHITECTS AND PLANNERS

DWORSKY ASSOCIATES
Architects and Planners

ESTABLISHED DATE
1953

ADDRESS
3530 Wilshire Boulevard
Suite 1000
Los Angeles, CA 90010

TELEPHONE
(213) 380 9100

FACSIMILE
(213) 380 7290

CHAIRMAN OF THE BOARD
Daniel L. Dworsky, FAIA

PRESIDENT
Robert L. Newsom, AIA

VICE PRESIDENT
Bruce M. Sellery, AIA

PRINCIPALS
Nathaniel M. Abrahms, AIA
Allan F. Dietel, AIA
Robert A. Levine, AIA
Robert Rosenberg, AIA
Gregory A. Serrao, AIA
Laurie B. Shaw
Wantland J. Smith, AIA, C.E.
Kenneth D. Stein, AIA
R. Michael Walden, AIA
Frank R. Webb, AIA

ASSOCIATES
Watana Charoenrath, AIA
Kip Dickson
Kathleen FitzGerald, AIA
Charmaine Howe, AIA
David Lai, AIA
Steve Kunin, AIA
Alix O'Brien, AIA
Kenneth Rossi, AIA

NUMBER OF EMPLOYEES
90

PROJECT TYPES
Commercial
Institutional
Interior Design
Multi-Use

CURRENT AND RECENT PROJECTS

Commercial
Research & Development Facility, American Honda Company
Neely Regional Office, Hewlett Packard Company
City Tower "The City", Tishman West Management Corp./Metropolitan Insurance
Engineering Office Building, The Aerospace Corporation
Loan Service Center, Home Savings of America
Long Beach Airport Center, Kilroy Industries
Westwood Terrace Office Building, Tishman West Management Corp.

Institutional
Los Angeles Municipal Court, Van Nuys Division
Los Angeles Branch, Federal Reserve Bank of San Francisco
Federal Building - Long Beach, General Services Administration
Engineering Building, San Jose State University
Student Health Center, California State University, Northridge
Theater Arts Building, California State University, Dominguez Hills
Civic and Cultural Center, City of Brea
County Government Center, County of Ventura
Westwood Recreation Community Center, City of Los Angeles

Interior Design
Screening & Reception Facility, Home Box Office
Federal Building - Long Beach, General Services Administration

Multi-Use
Angelus Plaza Elderly Housing, Retirement Housing Foundation
Skyline Condominiums/Metropolitan Apartments, Forest City Enterprises
Tom Bradley International Terminal, Los Angeles International Airport

EXPERIENCE
An architectural firm's experience combines the knowledge and skill gained from its completed projects and the background and contributions of each professional on the staff. Dworsky Associates' staff includes a high percentage of registered architects, each with unique skills and experience. The firm's completed work includes the architecture and planning of a diverse range of corporate, commercial, civic, cultural, academic, residential and technical projects.

Many of the projects designed by Dworsky Associates require specialized technical knowledge and understanding of functions, uses, systems, equipment and materials. Others require detailed market studies, in-depth site analyses, and complex review and approval processes. As a result of its experience, Dworsky Associates is fully able to meet these challenges. The firm's staff works with the client to find the best solution for each project, whether it is a sophisticated office building, a politically sensitive redevelopment project, an advanced research facility or one of the many other challenging building types in today's competitive marketplace.

Dworsky Associates' extensive experience ensures that the design of each building will not only be functionally efficient but aesthetically distinctive. More than fifty awards for professional excellence attest to the design quality of such diverse buildings as an international airline terminal; a Federal Reserve Bank; corporate office complex; and many more.

The skills acquired in over thirty-five years of practice and the firm's strong commitment to creative planning, design excellence and responsive service, will provide for continuing quality architectural and planning projects.

THE FIRM
Dworsky Associates has grown to a 90-person architectural firm providing services in the areas of design, planning, programming, feasibility studies, and interior design. In addition to a reputation for award-winning design, the firm has an equally outstanding track record in project management, particularly in the areas of scheduling and budget control. Dworsky Associates is proud of its record of sustaining long-term client relationships and feel it reflects the firm's commitment to service. Dworsky Associates has chosen to remain a medium-size firm to maintain this optimum service level.

The common characteristic shared by each of the firm's projects is a state-of-the-art solution tailored to the particular requirements of each client. These requirements typically embrace a broad range of issues, including demanding schedule performance such as fast track construction methods, inflexible economic constraints, specialized user program elements, and unique urban design or aesthetic considerations.

PERSON TO CONTACT
Daniel L. Dworsky, FAIA
Robert L. Newsom, AIA

Mayo Clinic Jacksonville,
Jacksonville, FL

400 South Hope, Los Angeles, CA

Beverly Center, Los Angeles, CA

One Mellon Bank Center,
Pittsburgh, PA

California State Capitol,
Sacramento, CA

NCNB National Bank of Florida,
Headquarters, Tampa, FL

Hawaii Prince Hotel, Honolulu, HI

Hyatt Regency at Reunion, Dallas, TX

Fluor Corporation Division
Headquarters, Houston, TX

ELLERBE BECKET

Directors (L-R) Los Angeles: J.S. Sterling, R. Tyler, D. Kohler, L.M. Naidorf, R.J. Nasraway and H.C. Wolf

ELLERBE BECKET
Architects

ADDRESS
Los Angeles Office
Colorado Place
2501 Colorado Avenue
Santa Monica, CA 90404-3585

TELEPHONE
(213) 207 8000

FACSIMILE
(213) 828 7726

DIRECTORS
Los Angeles

James S. Sterling, AIA
Director of Marketing
Robert Tyler, FAIA
Design Principal
Don Kohler, AIA
Director of Operations
Louis M. Naidorf, FAIA
Design Principal
Robert J. Nasraway, AIA
Director, Los Angeles Office
Harry C. Wolf, FAIA
Design Principal

PROJECT TYPES
Office Buildings
Hotel/Resort
Institutional
High Technology
Health Care
Public Assembly
Residential
Restoration/Renovation
Retail/Commercial

SERVICES
Architecture
Engineering
Interior Design
Urban Design/Planning

OFFICES
New York
Washington, DC
Chicago
Minneapolis/St. Paul
Kansas City
Los Angeles

PERSON TO CONTACT
James S. Sterling, AIA

Less than a decade after the turn of the century, Franklin Ellerbe founded, in St. Paul, Minnesota, a modest architectural and structural engineering practice. Over the years, the company grew, expanded to other cities, and achieved national prominence in the fields of health care, educational facilities, corporate structures, and public assembly projects.

Nearly sixty years ago, the Becket firm was established. First in Los Angeles and then with offices across the country, the firm developed an international reputation for its work on projects in major cities around the world – with particular emphasis on corporate facilities, high-rise office buildings and hotels.

In 1988 the firms merged, creating a new entity with offices in six cities employing over 800 professionals, projects in 45 states and 300 cities worldwide, and the planning and design of over $1 billion in construction annually. Ellerbe Becket is now one of the largest architectural firms in the United States with a new strength in size, depth of experience, and resources.

With this solid foundation, our goal for the next decade is the pursuit of architectural excellence. Great architecture gives purpose to our lives and pleasure to all who encounter it. We make architecture because we love it; this is meaningful to us, to those who engage us, and to those who engage our buildings.

Elliott + Associates Architects

1

2

1. Building renovation for the law offices of Durbin
   Larimore & Bialick
2. The Centennial Apartment Building, Woonsockett,
   Rhode Island
3. Interior design for Prime Time Travel Agency
4. National Cowboy Hall of Fame Travelling
   Exhibit Gallery
5. Stage Center Theatre Renovation

3

ELLIOTT + ASSOCIATES ARCHITECTS

(L-R): R. Elliott, D. Foltz, B. Yen,
J. Larson and J. Martin

ELLIOTT + ASSOCIATES ARCHITECTS

ESTABLISHED
1976

ADDRESS
6709 North Classen Blvd.,
Suite 101
Oklahoma City, OK 73116

TELEPHONE
(405) 843 9554

NUMBER OF EMPLOYEES
8

PROJECT TYPES
Corporate Offices
Financial Institutions
Historical Restoration/
Renovation
Law Offices
Medical
Museums
Restaurants
Retail

OTHER DISCIPLINES
Architectural, Interior and
Graphic Design
Renovation/Restoration

PERSON TO CONTACT
Rand Elliott, AIA

4

CURRENT AND RECENT PROJECTS
American Real Estate Group, Irvine, CA
Federal Express Corporation
GNA Insurance, Seattle, WA
IBM Corporation
OMRON
Oklahoma Tax Commission
Corken International Corporation
U.S. Marshals Foundation, Washington, DC
Stage Center Renovation (formerly The
Mummers Theatre)
Remington Park/Debartolo Corporation
OXY USA, INC.
Sonic Drive-In Restaurants
Southwestern Bell Telephone Company
D.P.W. Employees Credit Union
Bank of Oklahoma
Centennial Apartments, Woonsocket, RI
Days Inn Motels
National Cowboy Hall of Fame and Museum
Howard Weil Labouisse Friedrichs
Prime Cut Restaurants
Loomis Armored Car
Spaulding and Slye
The Economy Company/McGraw Hill
Ackerman Hood McQueen Advertising
The Midland Company

PROFILE
Rand Elliott, AIA
January 1989

*"We're often asked what we think makes
our projects so distinctively different from
one another. The answer, simply, is that at
Elliott and Associates we strive to create a
unique 'personality' for each project. That
'personality' is a combination of the
owner's desires, his marketing goals, and
our design intuitions.*

*You'll see an experimental nature to our
work, but in the sense that it reflects an
examination of things from new perspectives.
Our reputation has been built on a desire to
innovate. That, and our attention to
important, delicate details.*

*Essentially, at Elliott and Associates, we create
images for companies in the physical form.
And it's a challenging endeavor. When you're
helping to create an image for a company
you're drawing on experience you've gained
from past projects, developing appropriate new
ideas, and re-applying it all in new ways."*

The Centennial Project (2) is an 11 story
apartment building in Woonsocket Rhode
Island, set on a very interesting, rocky,
wooded site. A blending of natural, native
colors — the gray-green of a native stone,
along with accents of copper — fit the
building comfortably and contexturally with
its surroundings.

Our design, which made unnecessary the
expected entrance canopy, instead allows
automobiles to penetrate the building
through a grand, yet unobtrusive, central
portal. It is both a distinctive and functional
feature of the building.

The Durbin Larimore and Bialick
project (1) was for a young law firm, of
which one partner had inherited an old
apartment building -- virtually a family
heirloom. The challenge was to design a
complementary new addition without
destroying the architectural character of the
original structure. Our concept ties old to
new, sympathetically, and embraces the
history of the original structure.

The Prime Time Travel project (3) stems
from the concept that this travel agency is
selling otherworldly adventure. The sense of
the future is strong and the steamer chairs
are reminiscent of early steamship travel.
They lend an air of the past mixed with the
idea of the ultimate travel experience, space
travel.

5

Created by John Johansen, the Stage Center
Theater (5) is recognized around the world
as a work of art. New exterior and interior
lighting introduces a sense of drama and
excitement. A feeling that is enhanced
inside by the warmth and wonder provided
at 100,000 18" long pieces of string hanging
from the ceiling in all public areas.

The National Cowboy Hall of Fame
Travelling Exhibit Gallery (4) expresses the
simplicity of the American West and the
honesty of the people who lived there with a
common icon of the times: a sun-bleached
bison skull.

When you pass under this gateway you find
a memorable space that, as the cornerstone
for future renovations, will help redefine the
image of a fascinating treasury for part of
America's past.

Earl R. Flansburgh + Associates, Inc.

1. Rubin and Rudman, Boston, MA
2. Boston Design Center, Boston, MA
3. Boston Design Center, Boston, MA
4. Worcester Polytechnic Institute, Worcester, MA
5. Angell Memorial Park in Post Office Square, Boston, MA

EARL R. FLANSBURGH + ASSOCIATES, INC.

E. Flansburgh   M. Bourque

EARL R. FLANSBURGH + ASSOCIATES, INC.

ESTABLISHED DATE
1963

ADDRESS
77 North Washington Street
Boston, MA 02114

TELEPHONE
(617) 367 3970

FACSIMILE
(617) 720 7873

DIRECTORS
Earl R. Flansburgh, FAIA
Michael H. Bourque, IBD
Denis Boucher
Larry R. Carr
David S. Soleau, AIA

NUMBER OF EMPLOYEES
70

PROJECT TYPES
Corporate/Commercial
Educational Facilities
Housing
Renovation and Restoration

DISCIPLINES
Architecture
Graphic Design
Interior Design
Landscape Architecture
Master Planning
Space Planning

PERSONS TO CONTACT
Earl R. Flansburgh, FAIA
Michael H. Bourque, IBD

CURRENT AND RECENT PROJECTS

Corporate/Commercial
Ropes & Gray, Boston, MA
IBM Corporation, Waltham, MA
Wang Laboratories, Inc., Chelmsford, MA
Digital Equipment Corporation, Andover, MA
Fidelity Investments, Las Colinas, TX
Bank of Boston, Newton, MA

Educational Facilities
Harvard University, Boston, MA
Cornell University, Ithaca, NY
Boston University,
Wang Institute of Graduate Studies, Tyngsborough, MA
Jubilee School, Amman, Jordan

Housing
Edgewood Life Care Complex, North Andover, MA
Worcester Polytechnic Institute, Founders Hall Dormitory, Worcester, MA

Renovation and Restoration
Boston Design Center, Boston, MA
Boott Mill Restoration, Lowell, MA

DESIGN PHILOSOPHY AND HISTORY

Earl R. Flansburgh + Associates, Inc. is a multi-disciplinary design firm, offering comprehensive professional services in Architecture, Landscape Architecture, Space Planning & Interior Design, Master Planning, and Graphic Design. The firm has experience with a variety of project types; it has worked for developers and corporations, municipal and government agencies, and public and private educational institutions. In 25 years of practice, the firm has received over 60 national or regional design awards.

Design is approached as a collaborative effort, utilizing the talents and expertise of individuals from varied disciplines. This unique, interdisciplinary approach allows Earl R. Flansburgh + Associates, Inc. to concentrate a wide range of professional skills on the specific needs of each client. The firm's objective is to produce a sensitively crafted design which is responsive to each client's requirements while working within budget and schedule constraints.

Excellent design, creative planning, and technical expertise provide the basis of the design philosophy at Earl R. Flansburgh + Associates, Inc. The firm's diversity allows it to respond to the uniqueness of each project, creating spaces which work well functionally while projecting the image and values of the client.

FRANKFURT-SHORT-BRUZA ASSOCIATES, P.C.

FRANKFURT-SHORT-BRUZA ASSOCIATES, P.C.

ESTABLISHED
1945

ADDRESS
5701 N. Shartel, Suite 210
Oklahoma City, OK 73118

TELEPHONE
(405) 840 2931

OFFICERS
William W. Frankfurt
- President
Glenn E. Short
- Executive Vice President
Jim W. Bruza, AIA
- Executive Vice President
Gary L. Willis, AIA
- Vice President-Architecture

NUMBER OF EMPLOYEES
50

PROJECT TYPES
Commercial and Corporate Offices
Computer Centers
Industrial/Manufacturing Facilities
Medical Facilities
Research/Laboratory Facilities
Aircraft Maintenance Facilities

OTHER DISCIPLINES
Interior Design/Space Planning
Civil Engineering
Structural Engineering
Mechanical Engineering
Electrical Engineering
Fire Protection Engineering

PERSON TO CONTACT
William W. Frankfurt - President

CURRENT AND RECENT PROJECTS

Commercial and Corporate Offices
Conoco, Inc., Office Towers,
Ponca City, OK
Fleming Companies,
Corporate Headquarters,
Oklahoma City, OK
Hertz Corporation,
Oklahoma City, OK
Kerr-McGee Center,
Headquarters Building,
Oklahoma City, OK
Local Federal Savings & Loan,
Corporate Headquarters,
Oklahoma City, OK
Oklahoma Gas & Electric
Company, Oklahoma City, OK
Oklahoma Natural Gas
Company, Oklahoma City, OK
Scrivner, Inc.,
Corporate Headquarters,
Oklahoma City, OK

Computer Centers
Hertz World Wide Reservation Center,
Oklahoma City, OK
American Airlines, Computer Center,
Tulsa, OK

Industrial/Manufacturing Facilities
Westinghouse Manufacturing Plant,
Norman, OK
Mobil Chemical Company,
Manufacturing Plant, Shawnee, OK
Fife Corporation, Manufacturing Facility,
Oklahoma City, OK
General Electric Company, Warehouse
Facility, Oklahoma City, OK
Conoco, Inc., High Density
Polyethylene Plant, Alvin, TX

Medical Facilities
Baptist Medical Center, Oklahoma City, OK
The University of Oklahoma Health
Sciences Center, Oklahoma City, OK
Veterans Administration Hospital,
Oklahoma City, OK
General Leonard Wood Army Hospital,
Ft. Leonard Wood, MO

Research/Laboratory Facilities
United States Department of Energy,
High Explosives Applications Facility,
Livermore, CA
Kerr-McGee Corporation, Research Facility,
Oklahoma City, OK
Oklahoma State University, Noble Research
Center, Stillwater, OK

Aircraft Maintenance Facilities
American Airlines Maintenance/Overhaul
Base, Tulsa, OK
American Airlines Hangar 10 Addition,
JFK Airport, NY
American Airlines Maintenance Hangar,
Chicago O'Hare Airport, IL
American Airlines Hangar and Maintenance
Facility, Dallas/Ft. Worth Airport, TX
Braniff International Airlines Hangar and
Warehouse, Dallas/Ft. Worth Airport, TX
USAir, Inc., Maintenance Hangar and Shops,
Pittsburgh, PA
Three Bay Maintenance Hangar, B1B
Bomber Aircraft, Dyess Air Force Base, TX

DESIGN PHILOSOPHY

The architectural mission of Frankfurt-Short-Bruza Associates (FSBA) is embodied in the statement: "Bringing Life to Management through Construction." At FSBA we recognize that space based upon a management philosophy is fundamental to an efficient and effective building design. Our task is to define our client's method and style of management and reflect it in a space that satisfies function, aesthetic and practical requirements.

THE ART OF ARCHITECTURE

Architecture is one of the world's ancient art forms. It envelops light and shade, line and form, color and texture, style and function. How these elements are integrated reflects the abilities of the architect and mirrors the philosophy and feelings of the client.

The architects at Frankfurt-Short-Bruza Associates are licensed, award-winning professionals. The many design awards that FSBA has received bring credit to the architect and distinction to the client.

Our high quality design stems from an ability to identify and respond sensitively to the needs of the client. Through creativity, technical expertise, and a thorough knowledge of the building industry, our architects develop designs which satisfy both the functional needs and aesthetic values of our clients.

THE STRATEGY OF PLANNING

FSBA provides professional planning services for site planning, programming, space planning and special engineering studies. Site planning spans between the process of developing the proper relationship between a building and a specific site to the analysis of integrating multi-use developments within larger urban areas. It involves zoning legislation, building codes, neighborhood relations, visual impacts, traffic flow and control, and land use analysis. Programming is the preliminary examination of the space needs that the client will require in a proposed building. Space planning is the layout and assignment of areas within a structure through a synthesis of client needs and available space to meet the functional program.

THE TECHNOLOGY OF ENGINEERING

Engineering technology provides the knowledge to make functional a building's structure and its mechanisms. A properly engineered structure enhances design and increases the life and use of the building. It is the engineer who adds the necessary skills to make the various aspects of the building operate as an integrated unit. Although the work of the engineer is often subtle or unseen in the finished project, it provides the framework for creating a successful project of lasting high quality.

The engineers at FSBA represent the major disciplines of mechanical, electrical, structural, and civil engineering. These professionals have developed special expertise in the areas of fire protection, process piping, value engineering, and energy conservation.

Walt Disney Concert Hall

Walt Disney Concert Hall

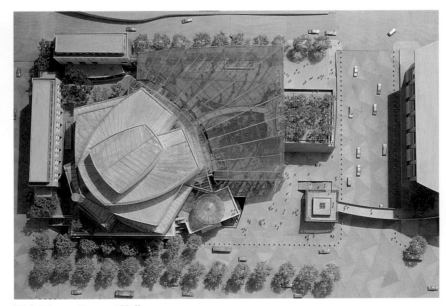

Walt Disney Concert Hall

FRANK O. GEHRY & ASSOCIATES

▲ Kobe Restaurant, Kobe, Japan ▼

FRANK O. GEHRY & ASSOCIATES

ADDRESS
1520-B Cloverfield Boulevard
Santa Monica, CA 90404

TELEPHONE
(213) 828 6088

FACSIMILE
(213) 828 2098

PRINCIPAL
Frank Gehry, FAIA

With Mr. Gehry as principal, Frank O. Gehry and Associates was established in 1962. During these 27 years of practice, the firm has received international recognition for its work and has won many awards. The firm's work has been published extensively and Mr. Gehry's drawings, models and furniture have been exhibited in museums in the United States, Europe and Japan. The firm's work is varied and includes many building types, most recently the California Aerospace Museum, the Loyola Law School, the Frances Howard Goldwyn Hollywood Regional Branch Library, Santa Monica Place and the Temporary quarters for the Museum of Contemporary Art in Los Angeles.

Current projects include a headquarters facilities for the advertising agency, Chiat-Day; a museum for Vitra International in Switzerland, the American Center in Paris, a restaurant in Kobe, Japan; and several large-scale mixed use projects in early stages of development. The firm continues to explore new design concepts in smaller scale residential projects and furniture design.

The firm is currently located in Santa Monica, California and has a staff of approximately thirty professionals.

1

3

2

4

5

6

7

8

1. The Grand Exchange Building,
   Kansas City, MO
2. Historic Navarre Building, Denver, CO
3. Schwegler Elementary School, Lawrence, KS
4. First United Methodist Church,
   Lawrence, KS

5. Telecommunications Tower, Lawrence, KS
6. Hall Kimbrell Corporate Office,
   Lawrence, KS
7. Hall Kimbrell Corporate Offices,
   Lawrence, KS
8. Historic Gumbel Building, Kansas City, MO

9. Chanute High School, Chanute, KS
10. Marvin Hall, University of Kansas,
    Lawrence, KS
11. National Weather Service, National Locations
12. Johnson County Central Library,
    Overland Park, KS

GOULD EVANS ARCHITECTS, P.A.

Robert E. Gould & David C. Evans

GOULD EVANS ARCHITECTS, P.A.

ESTABLISHED
1974

ADDRESSES
4600 Madison Ave., Suite 950
Kansas City, MO 64112
Telephone (816) 931 6655
Facsimile (816) 931 9640

706 Massachusetts Street
Lawrence, KS 66044
Telephone (913) 842 3800
Facsimile (913) 842 3830

PRINCIPALS
Robert E. Gould, AIA
David C. Evans, AIA

ASSOCIATES
Mark M. Miller, AIA
Rick G. Kanoy, AIA
Dennis R. Warnecke, AIA

NUMBER OF EMPLOYEES
30

PROJECT TYPES
Commercial
Office, Retail, Corporate, Urban
Development, Industrial
Educational
Higher Education, Secondary and
Elementary Schools, Child Care,
Master Planning, Classrooms,
Libraries, Laboratories
Government
Office/Computer Facilities,
Judicial, Armories
Recreational/Community
Museums, Libraries, Community
Centers, Gymnasiums
Religious
Churches, Private Schools
Residential
Houses, Apartment Complexes
Other Disciplines
Interior Design/Space Planning
Urban Design/Master Planning

CURRENT AND RECENT PROJECTS
(not pictured)
Commercial
Douglas County Bank, Lawrence, KS
Eldridge Hotel, Interiors, Lawrence, KS
Hallmark Cards Inc., Offices, Lawrence, KS
Marion Laboratories, Laboratories/Offices,
Kansas City, MO
Student Loan Servicing Center, Regional
Office, Lawrence, KS
United Telephone Systems, Inc., Offices,
Junction City, KS
World Savings and Loan Association Offices,
Shawnee, KS
Educational
Flint Hall, University of Kansas,
Lawrence, KS
New Southeast Elementary School II,
Kansas City, MO
Plumb Hall, Emporia State University,
Emporia, KS
Weber Hall, Kansas State University,
Manhattan, KS

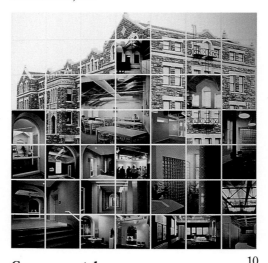

Governmental
GSA Office Building, Lawrence, KS
National Guard Armory, Boonville, MO
Riley County Courthouse, Manhattan, KS
Recreational/Community
Alvamar Racquet Club, Lawrence, KS
Community Center/Library/Senior Center,
Bonner Springs, KS
Community Center, Merriam, KS
Natatorium, Lawrence, KS
Senior Center, Lawrence, KS
Religious
Mustard Seed Church, Lawrence, KS
St. Paul's Episcopal Church and Day School,
Kansas City, MO
Residential
Historic Family Housing Units,
Ft. Leavenworth, KS
Neighborhood Revitalization, Lawrence, KS
Raintree Neighborhood, Lawrence, KS
Southview Apartments, Lawrence, KS

11

PROFILE
Gould Evans Architects, P.A. is a
professional architectural, urban design,
and interior design firm. Professional
services are currently provided in Kansas,
Missouri, and throughout the United States
from offices in Lawrence, Kansas and
Kansas City, Missouri. The firm is
continuously involved in a variety of projects
ranging from the specific design of interior
spaces to the overall planning for a central
business district. During the past 10 years,
Gould Evans Architects has received 22
awards recognizing their commitment to
technical and aesthetic excellence.

PHILOSOPHY
The firm is committed to a balance between
technical and functional efficiency, the social
and psychological needs of the clients and
occupants of the building, and aesthetic
quality. The firm's work does not reflect a
particular style but rather an effort to create
architecture that provides a pleasant place to
be. Each project represents an opportunity
to adapt a building to the surroundings of
either existing buildings in urban settings or
the open settings of suburban sites.

APPROACH
The principals, associates, and staff are
committed to a thorough and innovative
approach to planning and design. Each
project is approached as an on-going
interactive dialogue with clients where
alternatives are presented and evaluated on
the basis of overall costs and benefits. One
of the principals is responsible for and
coordinates all members of the professional
team. The firm offers a high degree of
professionalism, matched with a clear
understanding and appreciation for the
demands of each client.

1

2

3

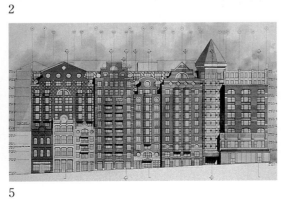

4

5

1. One Bowdoin Square Offices,
   Boston, MA

2. 75 State Street, Boston, MA
   (Graham Gund Architects and
   Skidmore, Owings & Merrill, Design
   Architects) © Steve Rosenthal

3. Church Court Condominiums,
   Boston, MA © Steve Rosenthal

4. One Faneuil Hall Square
   Offices, Boston, MA
   © David Hewitt

5. The Lansburgh's Residences
   and Arts Center,
   Washington, DC

6. Davidson College Visual Arts
   Center, Davidson,
   North Carolina © David Hewitt

GRAHAM GUND ARCHITECTS

Graham Gund

© Richard Howard

GRAHAM GUND ARCHITECTS

ESTABLISHED
1971

ADDRESS
47 Thorndike Street
Cambridge, MA 02141

TELEPHONE
(617) 577 9600

FACSIMILE
(617) 577 9614

PRINCIPALS
Graham Gund, FAIA
David Perry, AIA
Peter E. Madsen, FAIA

NUMBER OF EMPLOYEES
60

PERSONS TO CONTACT
Graham Gund, FAIA
David Perry, AIA

PROJECT TYPES

Commercial
Educational
Hotels
Housing
Institutional
Residential

HISTORY

Graham Gund Architects is a professional firm of 60 architects, designers, and landscape architects providing complete architectural, planning, and urban design services. GGA has in-depth, sophisticated technical staff, adept at building construction and detailing, specifications, and complete construction administration. Founded in 1971, the firm has produced a wide variety of critically acclaimed buildings.

The most successful plans and designs result from close attention to the client's goals and the interrelationship between the design, costs, scheduling, and technical considerations of construction. Graham Gund Architects' approach to design involves an analysis of the particular site and its context and unique features, as well as an understanding of the specific building program and goals for the project. The design process includes studies of various ideas to develop a design concept appropriate to the site and program.

Our approach to design is not a single, stylistic language, but a process that evolves into an aesthetic solution which incorporates the project's special qualities. The result is a project which is not only unique, but stimulating, innovative and contemporary.

CURRENT AND RECENT PROJECTS

Commercial
75 State Street, Boston, MA
One Faneuil Hall Square Offices, Boston, MA
One Bowdoin Square Offices, Boston, MA
South Hadley Town Center, South Hadley, MA
Waterville Valley Town Square, Waterville Valley, NH
Bulfinch Square Offices, Cambridge, MA

Educational
Mount Holyoke College Library, South Hadley, MA
Davidson College Visual Arts Center, Davidson, NC
Westminster School Performing Arts Center, Simsbury, CT
Connecticut College Admissions Building, New London, CT
Connecticut College Humanities Center, New London, CT
The School of the Boston Museum of Fine Arts, Boston, MA
Radcliffe College Research Center, Cambridge, MA
Carroll Center for the Blind, Newton, MA
Harvard University Johnston Gatehouse, Cambridge, MA

Institutional
Fernbank Museum of Natural History, Atlanta, GA
The Maritime Center (Museum, Aquarium, and Imax Theater) at Norwalk, CT
Lincoln Library, Lincoln, MA
Boston Ballet, Boston, MA
Visitor Center at Plimoth Plantation, Plymouth, MA
The Concord Museum, Concord, MA
Museum of American Textile History, Lawrence, MA
Boston Center for the Arts, Boston, MA
Arnot Art Museum, Elmira, NY
Institute of Contemporary Art, Boston, MA

Hotels
The Quincy Square Inn (Harvard University), Cambridge, MA
Lewis Wharf Hotel and Residences, Boston, MA
Waterville Valley Golden Eagle Lodge, Waterville Valley, NH
Hyatt Regency Hotel, Cambridge, MA

Housing
The Lansburgh Residences and Arts Center, Washington, DC
The Schoolhouse on Monument Square (Apartments), Charlestown, MA
Church Court Condominiums, Boston, MA
The School-House Condominiums, Boston, MA

6

The Humana Building, Louisville, KY. Photo Credit: William Taylor

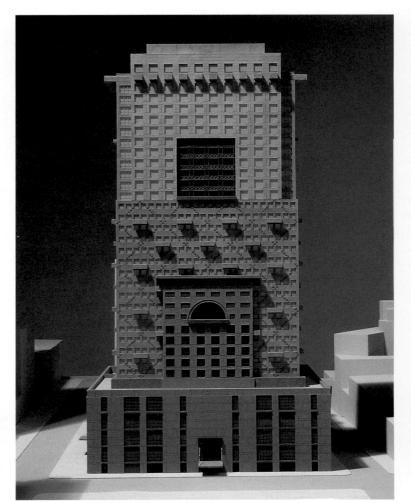

Sotheby's Tower New York, NY. Photo Credit: William Taylor

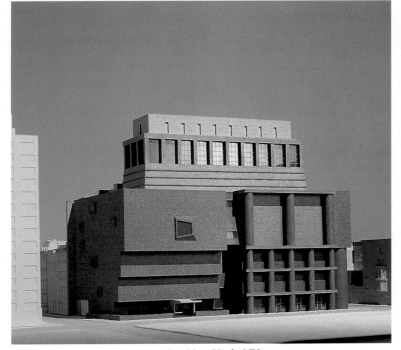

Whitney Museum of American Art, New York, NY. Photo Credit: William Taylor

Walt Disney World Dolphin and Walt Disney World Swan Hotels, FL.
Photo Credit: William Taylor

MICHAEL GRAVES, ARCHITECT

MICHAEL GRAVES, ARCHITECT

ESTABLISHED DATE
1964

ADDRESS
341 Nassau Street
Princeton, NJ 08540

TELEPHONE
(609) 924 6409

FACSIMILE
(609) 924 1795

NUMBER OF EMPLOYEES
70

PROJECT TYPES
High-rise offices, museums, university facilities, libraries, resort/convention hotels, private residences

OTHER DISCIPLINES
Urban design, interior design, furniture design, product design, graphic design

PERSON TO CONTACT
Michael Graves
Karen Nichols, Senior Associate

CURRENT AND RECENT PROJECTS
The Portland Building, OR - 1980*
Environmental Education Center, Jersey City, NJ - 1980
San Juan Capistrano Library, CA - 1980
Eleven Furniture Showrooms and Offices for Sunar Hauserman, New York, Chicago, Houston, Los Angeles, Dallas, and London - 1980-1986
Whitney Museum of American Art, New York, NY - 1981
Emory University Art Museum, Atlanta, GA - 1982
The Newark Museum, NJ - 1982
The Humana Building, Louisville, KY - 1982
Matsuya-Ginza Department Store, Tokyo, Japan - 1982
Riverbend Music Center, Cincinnati Symphony Summer Pavilion, OH - 1983
Ohio State University Visual Arts Center Competition, Columbus, OH - 1983
Mixed Use Development, Stamford, CT - 1984

Diane Von Furstenberg Boutique, New York, NY - 1984
Sotheby's Tower, New York, NY - 1984
West Virginia University Alumni Center, Morgantown, WV - 1984
Clos Pegase Winery, Calistoga, CA - 1984
Galveston East Beach Resort Master Plan, TX - 1984
Columbus Circle Mixed Use Development, New York, NY - 1985
Aventine Office Building and Hotel, La Jolla, CA - 1985
Shiseido Health Club, Tokyo, Japan - 1985
The Crown American Building, Johnstown, PA - 1985
Historical Center for Industry and Labor, Youngstown, OH - 1985
Disney Company Corporate Headquarters, Burbank, CA - 1985
Brisbane Civic Center, CA - 1986
Walt Disney World Dolphin and Walt Disney World Swan Hotels, FL - 1986
LJ Hooker Corporate Headquarters, Atlanta, GA - 1987
Henry House, Rhinecliff, NY - 1987
University of Virginia Arts and Sciences Building, Charlottesville, VA - 1987
City Centre Master Plan and Phase One Office Building, Los Angeles, CA - 1987
Apartment Building, Fukuoka, Japan - 1987
St. Marks Church, Cincinnati, OH - 1987
Condominium Tower, Yokohama, Japan - 1987
Parc de Passy Housing Competition, Paris, France - 1988
Lenox Stores and Boutiques - 1988
Sekisui House Office Building, Osaka, Japan - 1988
Sarah Lawrence College, Sports Center, Bronxville, NY - 1988
2101 Pennsylvania Avenue, Office Building, Washington, DC - 1988
Columbus Convention Center Competition, OH - 1989
Daiei Building, Yokohama, Japan - 1989
Detroit Institute of Arts Master Plan, MI - 1989
*Dates refer to date of commission

FIRM HISTORY

The office of Michael Graves, Architect was established in Princeton, New Jersey in 1964 and has completed a wide variety of projects, including institutional, cultural, and educational facilities, office buildings, urban development, hotels, and housing. The current staff of 70 people provides full architectural and interior design services. The firm has considerable expertise in helping clients at the earliest stages of projects by providing urban design, master planning, programming, space planning, and feasibility studies.

Michael Graves has great interest and abilities in the development of site strategies and contextual design. Graves is also well known for the design of murals, furniture, textiles, stagesets, and artifacts.

Michael Graves was born in Indianapolis in 1934. He received his architectural training at the University of Cincinnati and Harvard University. In 1960 Graves won the Rome Prize and studied at the American Academy in Rome, of which he is now a Trustee and member of the Society of Fellows. Graves is the Schirmer Professor of Architecture at Princeton University, where he has taught since 1962. He is a Fellow of the American Institute of Architects and is the winner of fifteen 'Progressive Architecture' design awards, seven American Institute of Architects National Honor Awards, and 30 New Jersey Society of Architects AIA Awards. The American Academy and Institute of Arts and Letters awarded Graves the Arnold W. Brunner Memorial Prize in Architecture in 1980. Numerous museums and galleries collect and exhibit his work; the Museum of Modern Art has presented Graves' work in eight exhibitions. Graves' work appears in many periodicals and books, including: 'Five Architects', published in 1979 by Academy Editions and Rizzoli; 'Michael Graves: Buildings and Projects 1966-1981', published in 1983 by Rizzoli; and 'Michael Graves: Buildings and Projects 1982-1988' to be released by Princeton Architectural Press in 1989.

DESIGN PHILOSOPHY

From the most complex program for urban buildings such as the Whitney Museum of American Art in New York and The Humana Building in Louisville, Kentucky, to the more rural settings of the Walt Disney World Hotels in Florida and the Clos Pegase Winery in California's Napa Valley, the Graves office has demonstrated an ability to design with a wide palette, sympathetic to both the general program and the local site context. In contrast to some recent abstract excesses of the Modern Movement, Graves' projects have attempted to make an architecture which expresses the more figurative and accessible symbols of our society. Graves recognizes that the users of buildings make natural associations through form, color, the composition of elements, and the hierarchical value of plans, all of which can give richer meanings to our inhabitation of buildings and the cultural artifacts surrounding us.

1. Manele Bay Hotel, Lanai Island
2. Mauna Kea Science Reserve,
   Master Plan, Hawaii Island
3. Mililani Town Center, Oahu
4. Embassy Suites at Wailea, Maui Island
5. 800 Fort Street Towers, Honolulu Harbor

GROUP 70 LIMITED

GROUP 70 LIMITED
Architects, Planners and Interior Designers

ESTABLISHED DATE
1971

ADDRESS
924 Bethel Street
Honolulu, HI 96813

TELEPHONE
(808) 523 5866

FACSIMILE
(808) 523 5874

PRINCIPALS
Francis S. Oda, AIA, AICP
- Chairman, CEO
Norman G.Y. Hong, AIA
- President, COO
Sheryl B. Seaman, AIA
Robert K.L. Wong, AIA
Hitoshi Hida, AIA

PROJECT TYPES
Resort Hotels
Commercial Office Buildings
Health Services Facilities
Educational Facilities
Governmental Facilities
Residential
Retail/Shopping Centers
Planning & Environmental Studies
Space Planning
Interior Design

CURRENT AND RECENT PROJECTS
Resort Hotels
Kawela Bay Hotels, Oahu
Manele Bay Hotel, Lanai
The Lodge at Koele, Lanai
Embassy Suites, Wailea, Maui
Embassy Suites, Poipu, Kauai
Maui Marriott Resort, Maui
Princess Hotel, Hawaii
Saipan Resort Hotel, Saipan
Iwasaki Capricorn Resort Hotel, Queensland, Australia
Sun Beach Lodge & Clubhouse, Okinawa
Plantation Suites Hotel, Kauai

Commercial/Retail
Tosei Office Building, Oahu
Iwasaki Sangyo Office Building, Kagoshima, Japan
800 Fort Street Towers, Honolulu Harbor
Mililani Town Center, Oahu
Daiei Hawaii, Oahu

Governmental
Naval Medical Branch Clinic, Pearl Harbor
University of Hawaii Physical Education Facility, Increments 1 & 2, Oahu
Mid-Level Astronomy Facility at Hale Pohaku, Mauna Kea
Chapel and Religious Education Facility, Pearl Harbor

Residential
Governor's Residence at Washington Place
Hawaii Loa Ridge, Oahu
Kaiser Marina Townhouses, Oahu
Academy Towers, Oahu
Villa Sampoerna, Kapalua, Maui

Planning & Environmental Analysis
Long Range Development Plan, University of Hawaii
Kapolei New Town Master Plan, Oahu
Kuilima Resort Master Plan, Oahu
Kaanapali Resort Master Plan, Maui
Lanai City Master Plan, Lanai
Mauna Kea Science Reserve Master Plan and Environmental Studies, Hawaii
Hawaiian Electric
- Facilities Master Plan, Oahu
East West Center Facilities
Master Plan, Oahu

Interiors
Manele Bay Hotel, Lanai
Beachcomber Hotel, Waikiki
Kona Lagoon Hotel, Hawaii
Keauhou Beach Hotel, Hawaii
First Federal Savings - Corporate Headquarters & Branches
Hawaiian Telephone Co. - Space planning
Hawaiian Electric - Space planning

COMPANY PROFILE
Group 70 Limited, established in 1971, is a major design firm in the Pacific. The winner of four significant design competitions in the past three years, the firm's achievements range from new city and world class destination resort planning to the design of internationally recognized hotels, metropolitan buildings, mixed-use commercial complexes and grand-scale residential developments. One of the largest design firms in Hawaii, Group 70 has been active in Hawaii, Australia, the Northern Marianas and Japan.

Cultural heritage and regional influences are emphasized in Group 70's design approach. In Hawaii, the firm coined the term "kamaaina architecture" to identify work that mirrors the 50th state's special ethnic blend. Projects undertaken in other Pacific communities are also reflective of the cultures within which they are developed.

Group 70 principals who take primary responsibility for capturing and characterizing each design's unique attributes, believe that the search for form is also a synergistic group process. This successful philosophy is rooted in the belief that clients deserve excellence at all levels of decision-making. The results are distinctive, award-winning environments that have rich appeal, harmony and increasing value over time.

HLM

2

3

5

4

1. Mercy Medical Plaza, Mercy Hospital
   Medical Center, Des Moines, IA
2 & 3. Olympia Place, Orlando, FL
4 & 5. The Christ Hospital Courtyard Atrium,
   Cincinnati, OH

HANSEN LIND MEYER INC.

HANSEN LIND MEYER INC.

Architecture•Engineering•Planning

DIRECTORS

John Douglas Benz, AIA
President
C. Bradford Bevers, AIA
Ronald J. Budzinski, AIA
John E. Carlson, AIA
Donald T. Finlayson, AIA
Thomas J. Kopecky, AIA
Chris E. Liakakos, AIA
Martin J. Meisel, AIA
Tom E. Thomas, AIA
Alan C. Wilson, AIA
James E. Zajac, AIA

ADDRESSES

Iowa City

C. Bradford Bevers, AIA
Managing Principal
Plaza Centre One
Drawer 310
Iowa City, IA 52244-0310
Telephone (319) 354 4700
Facsimile (319) 354 4707

Chicago

James E. Zajac, AIA
Managing Principal
Suite 1600
35 East Wacker Drive
Chicago, IL 60601-2102
Telephone (312) 609 1300
Facsimile (312) 609 0195

Orlando

John E. Carlson, AIA
Managing Principal
Suite 1100
800 North Magnolia Avenue
Orlando, FL 32803-3866
Telephone (407) 422 7061
Facsimile (407) 422 7066

ESTABLISHED

1962

NUMBER OF EMPLOYEES

400

Federal Correctional Institution,
Marianna, FL

DESIGN PHILOSOPHY

HLM believes in design excellence
which consistently blends aesthetics and
function. A proven approach evaluates a
range of alternative concepts with each
client and tailors design to match individual
needs. Clients benefit from the HLM
experience, ideas and services that lead to
timeless architecture.

**HLM is a full-service, interdisciplinary
firm.** Nationally recognized as an expert in
master facility and site planning, it
consistently produces high-quality, cost-
effective design—and creates the forms and
systems that give value to these designs.
For over 25 years, HLM has designed a wide
variety of projects ranging from simple
structures to complex technological
projects.

**HLM offers a team approach to project
management**, an organizational method to
provide services for individual projects.
Each project team nucleus is formed with a
principal-in-charge, a designer, an architect
and an engineer, as well as technical and
support personnel. These teams provide
continuous service from the earliest stage of
planning to building occupancy.

**HLM combines progressive business
principles with architectural practice**
and maintains a commitment to growth and
diversification. In addition to its regional
offices in **Iowa City, Chicago and Orlando**,
it has more recently developed offices in
New York City, Baltimore and Denver.
The resources and personnel of all HLM
offices are available to each client.

HLM is strongly dedicated to service and
values its long-term relationships. It views
repeat work as the best testimony for its
performance and experiences a high client
return rate.

PROJECT TYPES

Corporate/Commercial

HLM experience includes significant
projects in every area of this diverse market
segment. From highly customized and
elegant headquarter facilities to market-rate
office buildings, each is planned to allow
maximum flexibility for potential expansion
and commercial viability.

Criminal Justice

Justice architecture is one of the more
rapidly developing fields among HLM's
project types. The firm's knowledge of
operational considerations and evolving
corrections philosophies provides facilities
that run efficiently, safely, and at reduced
costs.

Health Care

HLM's attentiveness to each client's needs
and its emphasis on planning result in
facilities that are both functional and
attractive. Consistently ranked as one of the
top designers of Health Care facilities, HLM
helps clients market and deliver medical
services.

High Tech/Industrial

HLM's current assignments include major
university buildings, government agencies
and corporate centers. HLM blends
technological factors with psychological
considerations so people who use HLM
buildings benefit from a positive and more
productive environment.

Life Care/Housing

HLM designs each senior living facility for
the target market and is responsive to the
needs of the developer and the resident.
Work in this sector emphasizes a residential
scale and ranges from housing to retirement
communities.

REPRESENTATIVE CLIENTS

Corporate/Commercial

Olympia & York Southeast
Rockwell International
Searle Laboratories
Stepan Company
Schering-Plough, Wesley-Jessen

Criminal Justice

Bermuda Department of Public Works
Federal Bureau of Prisons
Florida Department of Corrections
Iowa Department of Corrections
Massachusetts Department of Corrections

Health Care

New York Health and Hospitals Corporation
Northwestern Memorial Hospital
Ochsner Medical Institutions
Orlando Regional Medical Center
Rush-Presbyterian-St. Luke's Medical Center
Shands Hospital, University of Florida
University Hospitals, University of Michigan
University of Iowa Hospitals & Clinics

High Tech/Industrial

Iowa State University
Johns Hopkins University School
   of Medicine
New York University
University of Illinois
University of Iowa College of Medicine

Life Care/Housing

Azalea Trace
Life Care Services Corporation
The Presbyterian Homes
Sisters of Charity
The Green Hills of Ames
United Methodist Homes of New Jersey

HARDY HOLZMAN PFEIFFER ASSOCIATES

HARDY HOLZMAN PFEIFFER ASSOCIATES

ADDRESSES
902 Broadway
New York, NY 10010
Directors: Hugh Hardy & Malcolm Holzman
Telephone (212) 677 6030
Facsimile (212) 979 0535

811 West 7th Street
Los Angeles, CA 90017
Director: Norman Pfeiffer
Telephone (213) 624 2775
Facsimile (213) 895 0923

FOUNDING PARTNERS
Hugh Hardy, FAIA
Malcolm Holzman, FAIA
Norman Pfeiffer, FAIA

MANAGING PARTNER
Victor Gong, AIA

NUMBER OF EMPLOYEES
100 (1988)

ARCHITECTURAL SERVICES
Corporate Development
Commercial Development
Educational/Institutional
Libraries
Visual Arts
Performing Arts
Restoration/Renovation/Adaptive Reuse
Mixed-Use Development

OTHER DISCIPLINES
Interior Design
Long Range Development
Master Planning
Programming/Space Planning

CURRENT AND RECENT PROJECTS

Corporate/Commercial Development
B. Altman's Midtown Centre, Renovation & Expansion, New York, NY (1991)
Tiffany Plaza Office Tower, New York, NY (1992)
Bryant Park Restaurants, New York, NY (1990)
Madison House Residential and Retail Tower, New York, NY (1992)
Wilshire/Maple Office Building, Los Angeles, CA (1993)
WCCO - Television Headquarters, Minneapolis, MN (1983)
BEST Products Corporate Headquarters (Phases 1 & 11), Richmond, VA (1980/1986)
Willard Intercontinental Hotel, Office & Retail Complex (Ext. Design), Washington, DC (1986)

Educational/Institutional/Libraries
Los Angeles Central Library, Renovation & Addition, Los Angeles, CA (1992)
Gurwin Educational Resource Center, Long Island Jewish Medical Center, New Hyde Park, NY (1991)
Student Activities Center, Middlebury College, Middlebury, VT (1990)
Darden School of Business, University of Virginia, Renovation & Additions, Charlottesville, VA (1992)
Science/Technology Building, State University of New York, Utica-Rome, NY (1988)
Wellesley College Sports Center, Wellesley College, MA (1985)

Visual Arts/Performing Arts Center
Performing Arts Center, Middlebury College, Middlebury, VT (1990)
Bowers Museum (Expansion), Santa Ana, CA (1990)
Alaska Center for the Performing Arts, Anchorage, AK (1988)
Robert 0. Anderson Building and Gilbert Decorative Arts Wing, Los Angeles County Museum of Art, Los Angeles, CA (1986/1992)
West Wing Addition, Virginia Museum of Fine Arts, Richmond, VA (1985)

Restoration/Renovation/Adaptive Reuse
The Plaza Hotel, Exterior Restoration & Addition, New York, NY (1992)
Los Angeles City Hall, Master Plan & Renovation, Los Angeles, CA (1990)
The Rainbow Room, Restoration, & Rockefeller Center Club, Reconstruction, New York, NY (1987)

Master Planning
Middlebury College, Middlebury, VT (1992)
Los Angeles County Museum of Art, Los Angeles, CA (1992)

PROFESSIONAL RECOGNITION
Individual Hardy Holzman Pfeiffer Associates' projects have merited numerous awards for excellence in both architecture and urban design. Architectural critics have also recognized the significance of the firm's work which is extensively presented in domestic and foreign publications. In addition to over 50 major honors for individual projects, HHPA has often received recognition for its work as a whole, as evidenced by the following major awards:

1981 Architectural Firm Award/ The American Institute of Architects
The HHPA citation for the highest honor the American Institute of Architects can bestow on an architectural firm reads: *"Designers of distinguished new structures, restorers of some of the finest treasures of an equally distinguished past...The success of their work is a testament to the values of experimentation and a collaborative spirit that responds with grace to the needs of a pluralistic society and the realities of the marketplace."*

1978 Medal of Honor/The New York Chapter, American Institute of Architects
The HHPA certificate for the Chapter's highest recognition cites: *"A partnership of complementary talents...Viewing the past and the present responsibly and freshly. Designing with ordinary parts to achieve extraordinary architectural results."*

1974 Brunner Prize in Architecture/ The National Institute of Arts and Letters
Given annually to an architect who has made a significant contribution to architecture as an art, the HHPA award reads: *"For their work which is civilized and urbane, and which has a full awareness of the past, a firm grip on the technology of our time, and something which has long been lacking in architecture -- a sense of humor. Yet it is executed with a seriousness of intention and a social awareness which are the marks of good building and great architecture."*

DESIGN PHILOSOPHY AND HISTORY
Since HHPA's inception in 1967 it has maintained consistently high principles in its approach to design: boldness, excitement, distinctiveness, liveliness, respect for surrounding environments, sensitivity to tradition. But most of all, the firm has sought to help clients express themselves in the spaces and forms created for them. HHPA's success has been in helping clients discover what their real objectives are, meeting challenges posed by existing circumstances, being responsive to institutional or corporate needs - both in the initial planning stages and through all stages of execution.

71

1

2

3

4

5

HARPER CARRENO INC.
SHWC HARPER CARRENO INC.

Harper Carreno Inc. Officers (L-R):
D.M. Harper, A.J. Carreno, C. Valdes-Fauli,
J.P. Davis and R.P. Hertig

HARPER CARRENO INC.
Architecture/Engineering

ESTABLISHED DATE
Harper Carreno Inc. 1979
SHWC Harper Carreno Inc. 1988

ADDRESS
8805 N.W. 23rd Street
Miami, FL 33172
Telephone (305) 593 0888
Facsimile (305) 593 1167

OFFICERS
David Michael Harper, AIA
- President & Chairman
Alberto J. Carreno, PE
- Executive V. P.
Carlos Valdes-Fauli, AIA
- Senior V. P.
John P. Davis, AIA - V. P.
Robert P. Hertig, AIA - Asst. V. P.
Katharyn E. Brodeur, - Asst. V. P.
Raymond C. Cook, PE - V. P.
Wayne V. Klassen, PE - V. P.
J. Luis Soro, PE - V. P.

SHWC HARPER CARRENO INC.

OFFICES
Miami, FL - David Michael Harper
Telephone (305) 593 0099
Dallas, TX - James W. Hiester
Telephone (214) 550 0700
Houston, TX - James W. Brown
Telephone (713) 875 6666
Reston, VA - David Wilson
Telephone (703) 648 1740

NUMBER OF EMPLOYEES
100-125 in Above Offices

JOINT VENTURE OFFICES
Tallahassee, FL - Jerry Hicks
Telephone (904) 893 1130

Hato Rey, Puerto Rico
- George McClintock
Telephone (809) 754 7745

PROJECT TYPES
Educational
Justice
Health Care/Laboratories
Commercial/Industrial

OTHER DISCIPLINES
Civil Engineering
Structural Engineering
Mechanical Engineering
Electrical Engineering

RECENT PROJECTS (From Opposite Page)

1. Kinloch Park Auditorium
A 1,000 seat circular Junior High School Auditorium renovation which included providing a complete new domed roof structure.

2. Southeastern College of Osteopathic Medicine
Multi-function building including library, student facilities, dining and tiered divisible lecture auditorium. The firm also provided the Master Plan for the campus which is located in North Miami Beach, Florida.

3. U.S. Coast Guard Base
Miami Beach, FL
Fast track design of five new buildings and 11.3 acre site including housing, medical, food service, exchange, club, maintenance shops, indoor firing range and recreational facilities. The project has received design awards for architectural excellence and is one of the nation's largest U.S. Coast Guard facilities.

4. Dade County Pretrial Detention Facility
National award winning project, located in Miami, Florida, provides 1,000 individual sleeping rooms within 26 self-contained housing units. The state of the art facility is one of the largest unit management jails in the United States.

5. State School "AAA"
Florida's largest high school providing Grades 9-12 and accommodating over 3,000 students. Located in Miami, the project is one of the first design/build schools in the United States.

HISTORY
In 1980 the firm was selected as the first prize winner to design the Regional Headquarters of the American Institute of Architects across from the Florida State Capitol in Tallahassee, Florida. During the past decade, the firm has continued to build upon a growing tradition of accomplishing important high visibility projects. Meeting the need for providing quality facilities for the public has been and continues to be a major element of the work of the firm.

The firm's commitment towards the design of Education Facilities led to the formation of the Educational Facilities Group which since 1983 has served continuously as Engineering Consultants to the School Board of Dade County for whom the firm has accomplished approximately 100 million dollars in projects. Recently, the firm joined with SHWC Architects to form the amalgamated firm of SHWC HARPER CARRENO INC. This specialty firm provides experience in the design of over one billion dollars in Educational Facilities during the past ten years. The firm's experience includes pioneering involvements in design/build schools such as planning and writing the R.F.P. for the 40 million dollar Middle School Program in Jacksonville, Florida.

In the specialty area of Architecture for Justice and secure facilities, the firm has designed numerous projects. Some recent examples include a Community Correctional Center Prototype which has been constructed in five metropolitan areas and has received a National citation for design excellence. Additionally, the firm has also designed the expansion of the largest Juvenile Justice Center in Florida and has been responsible for security analysis for the NASA Space Shuttle Program in conjunction with the design of the Alternate Central Security Control Center at Cape Canaveral.

The firm has served the public's need in the area of Health Care and Laboratories for repeat clients such as the Veterans Administration. Recent V.A. projects include conversion of existing buildings into research laboratories and building a new floor on top of an existing hospital to provide for a medical intensive care and coronary intensive care facility. Other recent laboratory projects include the design of the University of Florida Homestead Agricultural Research Center Campus.

Architecture for business and industry has also been an area of work by the firm. Projects such as the design of the Carnival Cruise Lines World Headquarters, along with other private sector work has included a wide variety of offices, shops, restaurants, computer centers, and industrial facilities.

1. Washington University Clinical Sciences Building, St. Louis
2. National Air and Space Museum, Washington, DC
3. St. Louis Union Station (renovation), St. Louis
4. BP America Corporate Headquarters, Cleveland
5. King Saud University, Riyadh, Saudi Arabia
6. King Khaled International Airport, Riyadh, Saudi Arabia
7. Hotel Nikko, Chicago
8. Temple, Reorganized Church of Jesus Christ of Latter Day Saints, Independence, MO
9. McDonnell Douglas Information Systems Group Computer Facilities, St. Louis
10. Levi's Plaza, San Francisco
11. Metropolitan Square, St. Louis
12. Dallas Galleria, Dallas
13. Houston Galleria, Houston

HELLMUTH, OBATA & KASSABAUM, INC.

HELLMUTH, OBATA & KASSABAUM, INC.
Architecture, Interiors, Planning, Graphics, Engineering

ESTABLISHED DATE
1955

ADDRESSES
Headquarters and St. Louis
Regional Office
1831 Chestnut Street
St. Louis, MO 63103
Telephone (314) 421 2000
Facsimile (314) 421 6073
Telex 44 7192

Dallas
6688 North Central Expressway
Dallas, TX 75206
Telephone (214) 739 6688

Hong Kong
Bank of America Tower
Suite 1401, 12 Harcourt Road
Hong Kong
Telephone (852) 5 227 168

Kansas City
323 West 8th Street
Suite 700
Kansas City, MO 64105
Telephone (816) 221 1576

London
HOK International Limited
New Oxford House
137 High Holborn
London WCIV 6PL England
Telephone (011) 44 1 831 7707

Los Angeles
1999 Bundy Drive
Suite 250
Los Angeles, CA 90025
Telephone (213) 207 8400

New York
641 Sixth Avenue, Sixth Floor
New York, NY 10011
Telephone (212) 741 1200

San Francisco
One Harrison Street
Suite 600
San Francisco, CA 94105
Telephone (415) 243 0555

Tampa
2502 Rocky Point Road
Suite 100
Tampa, FL 33607
Telephone (813) 887 5523

Washington, DC
1110 Vermont Avenue, N.W.
Suite 330
Washington, DC 20005
Telephone (202) 457 9400

PRINCIPALS
Gyo Obata
Chairman, President and Chief Executive Officer
King Graf
Vice Chairman - New Business Development
Jerry Sincoff
Vice Chairman - Operations
Robert Stauder
Vice Chairman - Administration and Finance

NUMBER OF EMPLOYEES
900

CONTACT PERSON
King Graf
Vice Chairman, New Business Development,
Corporate Headquarters

RECENT AND CURRENT PROJECTS

Corporate Headquarters
BP America (formerly SOHIO),
Cleveland, OH

Office and Commercial Buildings
Metropolitan Square, St. Louis, MO

Retail and Mixed Use Buildings
Dallas Galleria, Dallas, TX

Renovation
St. Louis Union Station, St. Louis, MO

Public and Institutional
National Air and Space Museum,
Washington, DC

Education
King Saud University, Riyadh, Saudi Arabia

Hotels and Conference Centers
Fairmont Hotel, Chicago, IL

Criminal Justice
Orange County Intake/Release Center,
Santa Ana, CA

Healthcare Facilities
University of Minnesota Hospital Renewal
Project, Minneapolis, MN

Research and Development Facilities
Washington University School of Medicine
Clinical Sciences Building, St. Louis, MO

Convention Centers
Taipei World Trade Center, Taipei, Taiwan

Transportation
King Khaled International Airport, Riyadh,
Saudi Arabia

Sports Facilities Group
Joe Robbie Stadium, Miami, FL

HISTORY AND DESIGN PHILOSOPHY
HOK is a highly diversified architectural design services firm founded by George Hellmuth, Gyo Obata, and George Kassabaum in 1955. From a staff of 26 people with projects concentrated in the American Midwest HOK has grown to an organization of about 900 employees with projects all over the world. It is the second-largest architecture, engineering, and planning firm in the U.S.

A subsidiary, the HOK Computer Service Corporation, markets software developed by HOK for computer-assisted design and drafting as well as for facility management.

HOK takes a multi-disciplinary approach to design, as reflected in the diversity of services the firm offers: architecture, engineering, planning, interior design, graphic design, landscape architecture, facility programming, and facility management.

From its inception, HOK has sought and won commissions for buildings of nearly every type. The firm's philosophy, as summed up by HOK Chairman Obata, is to *"solve problems posed by the space needs of people, and go beyond pure function to provide spaces that will enhance the lives of their occupants."* HOK does this by considering the needs of people first, then designing a project "from the inside out."

In every case, HOK is determined to approach each new commission without preconceptions. The firm also advocates a high level of client involvement. HOK believes this is essential to creating a design which is not only aesthetically pleasing, but also works in the real world.

HKS

1

2

3

4

5

1. Baylor University Medical Center,
   Dallas, TX
2. Kahi Mohala Psychiatric Hospital,
   Honolulu, HI
3. 100 Spear, San Francisco, CA
4. Lincoln Centre, Oakbrook
   Terrace, IL
5. Dominion Tower, Norfolk, VA

HKS INC.

HKS Executive Committee (L-R):
P.M. Terrill, Jr., C.J. Buskuhl, R.L. Shaggs
and R.M. Brame

HKS INC.
Architects Engineers Planners

ESTABLISHED DATE
1939

ADDRESSES
Dallas
1111 Plaza of the Americas North
LB 307
Dallas, TX 75201
Telephone (214) 969 5599
Facsimile   (214) 969 3397

Tampa
5401 W. Kennedy Blvd.
Suite 1090
Tampa, FL 33609
Telephone (813) 287 2140
Facsimile   (813) 286 8969

Los Angeles
912 N. La Cienega
Los Angeles, CA 90069
Telephone (213) 657 1283
Facsimile   (213) 659 8133

PRINCIPALS
Ronald L. Skaggs, FAIA
C. Joe Buskuhl, AIA
Ronald M. Brame, AIA
Paul M. Terrill, Jr., AIA
George R. Richie, AIA
John M. Bane, AIA
Jack R. Yardley, FAIA
J. Wade Driver, AIA
William B. Croft, AIA
Jack M. Nottingham, AIA
Ernest W. Hanchey, AIA
Robert H. Swaim, AIA, PE
E. Davis Chauviere, AIA
Keith J. Simmons, AIA
H. Ralph Hawkins, AIA
James L. Mitchell, PE
James B. Atkins, AIA
Noel Barrick, AIA
Robert E. Booth, AIA
John H. Richardson, PE
Joseph G. Sprague, AIA

NUMBER OF EMPLOYEES
380

PERSON TO CONTACT
Ronald L. Skaggs, FAIA
Chairman and Chief Executive Officer

PROJECT TYPES
Commercial
Office, Corporate, Hotel, Retail, Data Processing
Educational
School, College, University
Governmental
Civic, Correctional, Institutional
Health Care
Hospital, Ambulatory Care, Research,
Extended Care
Industrial
Manufacturing, Distribution, Warehousing
Recreational
Arena, Performing Arts, Sports Facility,
Auditorium

OTHER DISCIPLINES
Interior Design
Graphic Design
Facility Programming
Facility Evaluations
Master Planning
Facility Management
Computer Aided Drafting and Design
Model Services
Equipment Planning

CURRENT AND RECENT PROJECTS
Commercial
Greyhound Corporate Offices, Phoenix, AZ
MTech Center, Dallas, TX
Plaza of the Rockies, Colorado Springs, CO
Lincoln Plaza, Dallas, TX

Educational
Hughes-Trigg Student Center, Southern
Methodist University, Dallas, TX
Petroleum Engineering Building, Texas
A&M University, College Station, TX

Governmental
U.S. Postal Service Preferential Mail Facility,
Dallas, TX
Dallas County Jail Renovation, Dallas, TX

Health Care
Winchester Medical Center, Winchester, VA
Brooke Army Medical Center,
Fort Sam Houston, TX
St. John's Regional Medical Center,
Oxnard, CA
Pali Momi Medical Center, Honolulu, HI

Housing
888 Boulevard of the Arts, Sarasota, FL
USAA Towers, San Antonio, TX

Industrial
United Parcel Service, Little Rock, AR
Dallas Power & Light Company, Dallas, TX

Recreational
Las Colinas Inn and Sports Club, Irving, TX
Reunion Arena, Dallas, TX

PROFILE
Founded in 1939, HKS Inc. has executed
commissions for structures valued in excess
of six billion dollars.

During this fifty year period, HKS has grown
to be one of the largest architectural and
engineering firms in the United States, with
projects located throughout the nation.
Over two-thirds of HKS' current work is for
repeat clients.

HKS' business philosophy emphasizes
performance in achievement of client goals.
The deliberate and effective application of
this philosophy of service has resulted in the
ability to consistently deliver successful
projects that are well designed, technically
executed, and completed within budget and
on schedule.

DESIGN STUDIOS
HKS' design staff consists of a series of
design studios, each led by a principal
designer of proven talent and experience.
They place major emphasis on exploring
alternative concepts and encourage active
facility user participation. During
programming, planning, and design, equal
importance is placed on function, cost, and
schedule, with a belief that a balance of
these considerations provides the most
successful solution.

PROJECT MANAGEMENT
Project management is an HKS strength,
resulting both from the experience and
quality of its management personnel and
from its organizational structure. Project
managers have strong technical and
production backgrounds. They are
experienced in the tasks of project
execution, code compliance, scheduling,
coordination, detailing documentation, and
in the bidding and construction process.
They are specialists in "getting-it-done" well,
on time, and in budget.

COMPUTER SERVICES
HKS has steadily increased its use of
automated computer systems. Computer
services are routinely applied to basic office
activities, including project management,
scheduling, word processing, engineering
analysis, and specifications. Design studios
are aided by computer systems in providing
such services as space programming, cost
estimating and budgeting, adjacency
determination, and equipment planning.

Through the use of an extensive Computer
Aided Design and Drafting (CADD) system,
the firm has enhanced the speed, accuracy,
and completeness of its design activities and
production of construction documents.

HOWARD NEEDLES TAMMEN & BERGENDOFF

Partners (Top L-R): W. Love, C. Goodman
Associates (L-R): R. Jensen, R. Aarons,
E. Miller, R. Farnan, T. Williams, S. Reiss

HOWARD NEEDLES TAMMEN & BERGENDOFF
Architects Engineers Planners

ESTABLISHED DATE
1914

ADDRESSES
Kansas City
9200 Ward Parkway
Kansas City, MO 64114
Telephone (816) 333 4800
Telex   (816) 333 9327

Alexandria
Alexandria, VA 22314-1538
Telephone (703) 684 2700

Boston
Boston, MA 02199
Telephone (617) 267 6710

Indianapolis
Indianapolis, IN 46204-2135
Telephone (317) 636 4682

Los Angeles
Los Angeles, CA 90005
Telephone (213) 386 7070

Milwaukee
Milwaukee, WI 53224
Telephone (414) 359 2300

New York
New York, NY 10001-5086
Telephone (212) 613 5400

Phoenix
Phoenix, AZ 85016
Telephone (602) 954 7420

Seattle
Bellevue, WA 98004
Telephone (206) 455 3555

PERSON TO CONTACT
Mr. Bill Love, FAIA - Los Angeles
Mr. Cary Goodman, AIA - Kansas City
(Or any associate)

DIRECTORS
William Love, FAIA
Gary C. Goodman, AIA
Ross L. Jensen, AIA
Ronald W. Aarons, AIA
Ewing H. Miller, FAIA
Richard L. Farnan, AIA
Thomas L. Williams, AIA
Steven H. Reiss, AIA

NUMBER OF EMPLOYEES
2,200

PROJECT TYPES
Airport Facilities
Convention Centers
Educational Facilities
Health Facilities
Historic Renovation
Hotel/Hospitality
Interior Architecture
Office Buildings
Specialty Sports Facilities
Stadiums and Arenas

OTHER DISCIPLINES
Mechanical, electrical, structural
engineering, Urban Design & Planning,
Landscape Architecture, Graphic Design,
Construction Services

CURRENT & RECENT PROJECTS
Airport Facilities
Evansville Regional Airport, Evansville, IN
Charleston International Airport,
Charleston, SC

Convention Centers
Anaheim Convention Center, Anaheim, CA
Palm Springs Convention Center,
Palm Springs, CA

Education Facilities
Project Management Team, Kansas City,
Missouri School District, Kansas City, MO
Cibola High School, Yuma, AZ

Health Facilities
Holy Cross Hospital, Salt Lake City, UT
Saint Cabrini Hospital, Seattle, WA

Historic Renovation
Lincoln and Jefferson Memorials,
Washington, DC
Circle Theatre, Indianapolis, IN

Hotels
Doubletree Hotel, Santa Clara, CA
Irvine Hilton Hotel, Irvine, CA

Interiors
U.S. West Communications, Phoenix, AZ
Central States Pension Fund, Chicago, IL

Office Buildings
AT & T Town Pavilion, Kansas City, MO
Indiana State Office Building II,
Indianapolis, IN
APS Building at Arizona Center,
Phoenix, AZ

Stadiums and Arenas
B.C. Place Stadium, Vancouver,
British Columbia
The Hoosier Dome, Indianapolis, IN
(with BDPM Architects)
Fenway Park Renovations, Boston, MA
Baltimore Arena Renovation,
Baltimore, MD

Specialty Sports Facilities
Olympic Velodrome, Athens, Greece
Texas Rangers Spring Training Facility,
Charlotte County, FL

HISTORY/DESIGN PHILOSOPHY
Beginning with the acquisition of Kivett and
Myers, the architectural practice of Howard
Needles Tammen & Bergendoff (HNTB)
has grown into one of the country's top
architectural practices. Now celebrating its
75th anniversary, HNTB offers clients
comprehensive services from a single
design source.

HNTB recognizes that meeting high-design,
economic and functional expectations
demands the coordination and integration of
diverse and specialized skills. Committed to
the concept of total design, HNTB provides
full architectural services.

HNTB uses state-of-the-art technology to
plan and design facilities ranging from office
buildings, airports, sports facilities, hotels
and health facilities to convention centers
and industrial plants. HNTB provides
image-building projects, built with close
attention to detail and to the client's unique
requirements.

Innovative, functional and aesthetic design
solutions are the hallmark of HNTB.
Personal client attention, backed by HNTB's
network of offices nationwide, results in
efficient, cost-effective and timely services
for both the private and public sectors.

Seventh Market Place, Los Angeles, CA

Westside Pavilion, Los Angeles, CA

Horton Plaza, San Diego, CA

Fashion Institute of Design and Merchandising, Los Angeles, CA

1984 Olympics, Los Angeles, CA

THE JERDE PARTNERSHIP INC.

THE JERDE PARTNERSHIP INC.

ESTABLISHED DATE
September, 1977

ADDRESS
909 Ocean Front Walk
Venice Beach, CA 90291

TELEPHONE
(213) 399 1987

FACSIMILE
(213) 399 1664

PRINCIPALS
Jon A. Jerde, AIA - President
Eddie S.Y. Wang, AIA - Vice President
William De Eiel, AIA - Director of Design
Robert Cloud, AIA
Fred A. DeNisco, AIA
Charles E. Pigg
Paul N. Senzaki, AIA

NUMBER OF EMPLOYEES
80

PROJECT TYPES
Urban Planning
Commercial
Retail
Mixed-use
Athletic

PERSON TO CONTACT
Eddie S.Y. Wang, AIA - Vice President

CURRENT AND RECENT PROJECTS

Camelot,
Heathrow, FL
Circle Center,
Indianapolis, IN
EuroPark,
Mougins, France
Hollywood Promenade,
Hollywood, CA
Horton Plaza,
San Diego, CA
Kanebo Waterfront,
Fukuoka, Japan
Luminaire Houston,
Houston, TX
Main Place,
Santa Ana, CA
Mall of America,
Minneapolis, MN
Metropolis/Times Square,
New York, NY
1984 Olympics,
(ephemeral graphics and structures)
Los Angeles, CA
Paseo Alcorta,
Buenos Aires, Argentina
Princes Wharf,
Auckland, New Zealand

Seventh Market Place
Los Angeles, CA

Seventh Market Place has played a key role in the re-emergence of Downtown Los Angeles. Commissioned by Citicorp Plaza, this 70,000 square feet "urban grotto" sinks below street level between three skyscrapers.

Two major department stores connect at each level to a circle of storefronted balconies serviced by outdoor escalators and roofed by a spectacular spotlit steel trellis. Open metalwork gazebos house an elevator and kiosks, creating one of Jerde's "human, public spaces" for meeting and greeting. This project provides a stimulating urban experience and an example of successful merchandising.

Westside Pavilion
Los Angeles, CA

Four distinctly colorful pavilions characterize the Westside Pavilion. A block-long shopping mall in a prosperous residential neighborhood, Westside Pavilion's size is modified by eclectic architecture. Modelled after the European gallerias, the lively indoor street features a curved, continuous skylight, sunlit arcades on three levels offering a wide range of shopping, a multiplex cinema and a supermarket. Westside Pavilion sets the standard for a new generation of sophisticated malls.

Horton Plaza
San Diego, CA

Brightly colored and dramatically detailed, Horton Plaza, with its international flavor, acts as a potent catalyst for the revival of this downtown area. With a hotel, cinema complex, office spaces, parking garages and 165 specialty shops and restaurants, Horton Plaza has become a leading visitor attraction for the area.

1984 Olympic Games
Los Angeles, CA

During two magical weeks Los Angeles was transformed into one huge festival. The designers developed a "kit of parts" to tie the sprawling metropolis together. A unified theme of lightweight structures, signage, tenting and banners along with a palette of vivid colors united the scattered stadiums and campuses. The result was the creation of a range of "people places" that reached out and touched participants and viewers throughout the world.

1

3

1. Highway 111 Corridor - Master Plan, Indian Wells, CA
2. Giorgio Retail Store, Beverly Hills, CA
3. 1999 Avenue of the Stars, Los Angeles, CA
4. Opus One Winery, Napa, CA
5. Rincon Center, San Francisco, CA
6. Fox Plaza, Los Angeles, CA

JOHNSON FAIN AND PEREIRA ASSOCIATES

R. S. Johnson   W.H. Fain, Jr.

JOHNSON FAIN AND PEREIRA ASSOCIATES

ESTABLISHED DATE
1931

ADDRESS
6100 Wilshire Boulevard
Los Angeles, CA 90048

TELEPHONE
(213) 933 8341

FACSIMILE
(213) 933 3120

PRINCIPALS
R. Scott Johnson
- Design Partner
William H. Fain, Jr.
- Managing Partner

ASSOCIATES
Larry R. Ball
John R. Frost
Mark R. Gershen
Daniel J. Janotta
Paul A. Murphey
Robert Pigati
Ralph M. Stanislaw
Dianna Wong

NUMBER OF EMPLOYEES
60

PROJECT TYPES
Corporate/Office
Mixed-Use/Retail
Hotel/Resort
Educational
Governmental
Residential

DISCIPLINES
Architecture
Urban Design
Planning
Interior Design

CURRENT AND RECENT PROJECTS
(Partial listing)

Corporate/Office
Fox Plaza, Century City, CA
Construction Cost $90m.
1999 Avenue of the Stars,
Century City, CA
Construction Cost $90m.
Citicorp Center,
San Francisco, CA
Construction Cost $70m.

American Airlines Headquarters, Dallas-Fort Worth, TX. Construction Cost $41.5m.
Toyota National Headquarters, Torrance, CA
Construction Cost $40m.
Pasadena Towers, Pasadena, CA
Construction Cost $40m.
Lockheed Corp. Headquarters,
Calabasas, CA. Construction Cost $36m.
Carnation Plaza, Glendale, CA
Construction Cost $35m.
Transamerica Headquarters,
San Francisco, CA. Construction Cost $30m.
Avery Corp. Headquarters, Pasadena, CA
Construction Cost $12m.
Andrex Vermont Gateway, Torrance, CA
Construction Cost $12m.
William Morris Rodeo, Beverly Hills, CA
Construction Cost $8m.

Mixed-Use/Retail
Rincon Center, San Francisco, CA
Construction Cost $65m.
Laurel/Fifth Avenue, San Diego, CA
Construction Cost $40m.
Giorgio Retail Store, Beverly Hills, CA
Construction Cost $5m.

Hotel/Resort
The Registry Hotel, Universal City, CA
Construction Cost $78m.
Doha Sheraton, Doha, Qatar
Construction Cost $150m.
Miyama Hills Resort, Guam
Construction Cost $750m.
Makaha Valley Inn & Country Club,
Oahu, HI. Construction Cost $4.6m.
The Westin St. Francis Hotel,
San Francisco, CA. Construction Cost $20m.

Planning/Urban Design
Highway 111 Corridor - Urban Design Study,
Indian Wells, CA. 3.5 mile Corridor.
Unocal Property - Master Plan,
Los Angeles, CA. 18 acres.
Shaumburg Redevelopment Plan,
Schaumburg, IL. 237 acres.
Ewa Town Center, Oahu, HI. 6,000 acres.
Paramount Pictures - Master Plan,
Los Angeles, CA. 124 Bldg. Complex.
Calabasas Park Center, Calabasas, CA. 67 acres.
New District of Doha, Doha, Qatar. 5,000 acres.
Queen Mary Seaport, Long Beach, CA
100 acres.
Irvine Ranch, Orange County, CA. 93,000 acres.
University of California, Irvine, CA. 1,000 acres.

Governmental
Tom Bradley International Terminal,
Los Angeles International Airport
Construction Cost $123m.
Camp Pendleton Naval Hospital, Camp
Pendleton, CA. Construction Cost $30m.
Terminal Island Medical Clinic,
San Pedro, CA. Construction Cost $5m.
Veterans Administration Medical Clinic,
Fresno, CA. Construction Cost $5m.

Residential
The Chartwell Estate, Bel Air, CA
Construction Cost $30m.
The Courtyard, San Diego, CA
Construction Cost $52m.
Park Wellington, Los Angeles, CA
Construction Cost $8m.

Educational
Otis Art Institute of Parsons, School of
Design, Los Angeles, CA. Construction Cost $10m.
"Main Street" Urban Design Plan,
University of California, Irvine, CA
Whittier College Master Plan,
Whittier College, Whittier, CA
Pepperdine University, Malibu, CA
Construction Cost $25m.
Central Library, University of California,
San Diego, CA. Construction Cost $4.5m.
Medical Center, University of California,
Irvine, CA. Construction Cost $12m.
Nelson Research Center, University of
California, Irvine, CA. Construction Cost $5m.
Fred L. Hartley Research Center, Brea, CA
Construction Cost $30m.

DESIGN PHILOSOPHY/HISTORY
During almost 60 years of professional activity in the United States and overseas, Johnson Fain and Pereira Associates has established itself as an architecture and planning office known for its creative approach to the design of buildings, building complexes and new communities. R. Scott Johnson, Design Partner, and William H. Fain, Jr., Managing Partner, lead a diversified office of sixty professionals. Each project is carefully designed to specific client needs, program, and technical requirements in the context of community objectives. Every assignment presents the opportunity to develop a uniquely appropriate design solution. This philosophy is fundamental to the firm.

Our primary design objective is to identify and resolve the specific issues posed by each assignment. Particular emphasis is placed upon defining not only project scope and intent, but also budget and schedule at the inception of the design process. Attention to all levels of detail and close client communication continue throughout the duration of the project, to ensure the best possible match of the client needs, design intent and cost effectiveness.

The design of commercial office buildings, hotels, retail centers, medical and industrial facilities, academic and public buildings all receive the same high level of attention. In planning and urban design, new town plans, master plans for university, recreational, aviation and residential projects, as well as site feasibility and land use analyses are approached in a similarly thoughtful, responsive and analytical manner.

ARCHITECTS

1

2

1. First Union Branch Bank, Charlotte, NC
2. NCNB Plaza, Dallas, TX
3. Atlanta Midtown, Atlanta, GA
4. One First Union Center, Charlotte, NC
5. Southwestern Bell Telephone Company, Texas Headquarters, Dallas, TX

3

4

5

JPJ ARCHITECTS, INC.

Principals (L-R): W. Viney, R. Morgan, W. Nash, B. Smith, D. Atteberry, E. Spaeth, and W. Workman

JPJ ARCHITECTS, INC.
Architects and Interior Designers

ESTABLISHED DATE
1962

ADDRESS
5910 N. Central Expressway
Suite 1200
Dallas, TX 75206

TELEPHONE
(214) 987 8000

FACSIMILE
(214) 987 8099

DIRECTORS
Bill D. Smith, FAIA
Walter J. Viney, AIA
William H. Workman, AIA
Richard E. Morgan, AIA
Everett D. Spaeth, AIA
David L. Atteberry, AIA
Weldon W. Nash, FCSI, CCS

NUMBER OF EMPLOYEES
60

PROJECT TYPES
Corporate Facilities
Educational Facilities
Health Care Facilities
Religious Facilities
Office Buildings
Hotels

PERSON TO CONTACT
Bill D. Smith, FAIA - President

CURRENT AND RECENT PROJECTS

Corporate Facilities
Southwestern Bell Texas Headquarters, Dallas, TX for Southwestern Bell Telephone Company

Electronic Data Systems Command Center, Plano, TX for Electronic Data Systems

Southwestern Bell Communications Center, St. Louis, MO for Southwestern Bell Telephone Company

Dallas Power and Light Company Masterplan, Dallas, TX for TU Electric Company

Office Buildings
One First Union Center, Charlotte, NC for Childress Klein Properties

NCNB Plaza, Dallas, TX for Bramalea, Ltd., Toronto, Canada and PIC Realty

Atlanta Midtown, Atlanta, GA for Childress Klein Properties

300 Galleria, Atlanta, GA for Trammell Crow Company

Hotels
Hyatt Regency Fort Worth, Fort Worth, TX for Woodbine Development Corporation

Omni Charlotte Hotel, Charlotte, NC for Childress Klein Properties

Healthcare Facilities
Methodist Medical Center Patient Tower, Dallas, TX for Methodist Hospitals of Dallas

Methodist Medical Center Ambulatory Outpatient Services/Professional Office Building, Dallas, TX for Methodist Hospitals of Dallas

Methodist Medical Center Magnetic Resonance Imaging (MRI) Facility, Dallas, TX for Methodist Hospitals of Dallas

Charlton Methodist Hospital Ambulatory Care Center Labor/Delivery Facility, Dallas, TX for Methodist Hospitals of Dallas

Juliette Fowler Homes/Intermediate Care Facility, Dallas, TX for Juliette Fowler Homes

Southeastern Methodist Hospital CT-Scan Facility, Dallas, TX for Methodist Hospitals of Dallas

HISTORY
JPJ Architects, Inc. is a Dallas-based professional services firm engaged in the practice of architecture and interior architecture on a national scale, serving clients with a depth of experience that spans a broad range of building types, including office buildings, corporate headquarters, data centers, hotels and facilities for worship, health care, and education.

Founded as a partnership in 1962, the 60 person firm was incorporated in 1980 and is currently owned and managed by seven principals who share a commitment to the highest standards of professional service and design quality. The firm's work has been recognized for design excellence and technical proficiency through numerous publications and awards.

JPJ Architects approaches each project with the benefit of experience-based expertise, but without preconceived solutions. In collaboration with the client, the firm pursues carefully determined objectives as a highly organized and multi-disciplined design team supported by advanced computer technology. Specialized internal management systems are in place to achieve high levels of performance and efficiency throughout the project. Specialists seek to balance all project parameters and budgetary constraints within a context of resourcefulness and creativity. The result is an architecture of enduring appeal and unfailing suitability for its prescribed use.

Services offered include:
Architectural Programming
Feasibility Studies
Master Planning
Schematic Design
Design Development
Cost Estimating
Construction Documents Preparation
Bidding or Negotiation Assistance
Administration of the Construction Contract
Interior Design
Record Document Preparation

Special Services offered include:
Investigation of Existing Conditions
Equipment Surveys and Inventories
Site Evaluations
Financial Feasibility Studies
Needs Analysis Studies
Systems Evaluations
Special Consultant Coordination
"Financing Package" Preparation
Renderings/Architectural Models
CADD Simulation
Art Programs Coordination
Tenant Space Planning
Marketing Materials and Preparation
Extended Construction Administration
Moisture Protection Technology

1

2

3

1. Republic Place
2. PHICO Corporate Headquarters
3. Washington Design Center

KEYES CONDON FLORANCE ARCHITECTS

KEYES CONDON FLORANCE ARCHITECTS

ESTABLISHED DATE
1956

ADDRESS
1320 19th Street, N.W.
Washington, DC 20036

TELEPHONE
(202) 293 6800

FACSIMILE
(202) 296 9760

PRINCIPALS
Arthur H. Keyes, Jr., FAIA
David H. Condon, FAIA
Colden Florance, FAIA
Tam D. Nguyen, AIA
Thomas N. Eichbaum, AIA
Philip A. Esocoff, AIA
David R.H. King, AIA
Bruce W. Dicker, AIA
Russell K. Perry, AIA
Mark J. Maves, AIA

NUMBER OF EMPLOYEES
100

SERVICES
Architecture
Master Planning
Landscape Architecture
Interior Design
Feasibility Studies
Programming
Space Planning
Historic Structures Analysis
Environmental Impact Studies

PERSON TO CONTACT
Gary P. Fleming
Director of Marketing

REPRESENTATIVE PROJECTS

Mixed-Use/Commercial
2401 Pennsylvania Avenue
1100 New York Avenue
Washington Design Center
Republic Place
Torpedo Factory Waterfront Center
King Street Station

Corporate and High Technology
IBM Federal Systems Division
Headquarters
Smithsonian Museum Support Center
1st American Bank Headquarters
PHICO Corporate Headquarters

Educational Facilities
University of Maryland College of Business
& Management and School of Public Affairs
George Washington University National
Law Center
George Mason University School of
Business and Public Policy
The American University Tenley Campus

Museums
National Gallery of Art West Building
Renovations
National Museum of Women in the Arts
National Building Museum/U.S. Pension
Building Renovation

Master Planning
Pentagon Area Master Plan
Southeast Federal Center Master Plan
George Washington University Northern
Virginia Campus Master Plan

PROFILE

Architecture is not inherently simple. But at times, the temptation to categorize firms, or reduce the practice itself to a system, has been irresistible. In the 1960's for instance, predictions found architecture becoming more and more specialized, with building problems headed for simple, standardized solutions. A taste for complexity in architecture seemed no more than a designer's preference.

Today's building industry professionals would agree that complexity has become more than an aesthetic preference — it's now a fact of corporate and institutional life. Sites are tighter, old buildings must live new lives, and regulations, review boards and people in general have much more to say about how buildings are made and used. In this new environment, the best of the generalist, multi-service architecture firms have proven remarkably resilient in responding to changing times and issues.

Keyes Condon Florance is such a firm. Since its beginnings in 1956, KCF has built a tradition of architectural excellence with special talent and versatility. For more than thirty years, the firm has maintained a consistent record of high quality design while meeting the needs of developers, corporations, institutions and government agencies alike.

Today, we are both an established firm and one that constantly generates fresh ideas — the result of a planned transition from founding partners to younger leadership. And with diverse projects on the boards for nationally recognized private and public clients, the scope and variety of our work continue to grow.

While notable for innovation, our design approach is also characterized by detailed attention to owner objectives and a keen sensitivity to project contexts. At the same time, the structuring of management responsibilities allows each project team to provide the strong personal service necessary for meticulous quality control. The result is a distinctive solution, based on original thinking, for every assignment.

In our sophisticated economic and design era, the work of Keyes Condon Florance stands out as imaginative, practical and reliable — a balance that has earned the firm not only seventy-plus awards, but an equally long list of satisfied, repeat clients.

LANGDON WILSON ARCHITECTS PLANNERS

LANGDON WILSON
Architects Planners

ADDRESSES
Los Angeles
1055 Wilshire Blvd., Suite 1500
Los Angeles, CA 90017
Telephone (213) 250 1186
Facsimile   (213) 482 4654
Contact: Randy Jefferson

Orange County
4100 MacArthur Blvd., Suite 200
Newport Beach, CA 92660
Telephone (714) 833 9193
Facsimile   (714) 833 3098
Contact: Rick Poulos

Phoenix
3001 North Second Street
Phoenix, AZ 85012
Telephone (602) 241 0021
Facsimile   (602) 274 5593
Contact: Mike Schroeder

PARTNERS
Ernest C. Wilson, Jr., AIA
Jon Patrick Allen, AIA
Jack E. Camp, Jr.
Randolph A. Jefferson, MRAIC
Asad Khan
Vickers G. Marovish
Richard W. Poulos, AIA

ASSOCIATE PARTNERS
Dennis E. Ackel, AIA
Mario G. Ascarrunz, AIA
James D. Black, AIA/AICP
Richard A. Gardner, AIA
Gene Hamilton Klow, AIA
Vano Haritunians, AIA
James D. House, AIA
Michael C. Schroeder, AIA
Richard D. Sholl, AIA
Paul A. Thometz, AIA
Reynaldo V. Tuazon, AIA
Nien-Tsu Yuh, AIA

SERVICES
Architecture
Urban and Master Planning
Interior Design and Space Planning
Medical Planning and Design
Graphics

EXPERIENCE
The following projects represent the diversity of Langdon Wilson's expertise in the development of projects ranging in scale from several million square feet to less than 100,000 square feet:

Master Planning
Koll Center Irvine North, CA
Sierra Point, CA
Irvine Spectrum, CA
Goodyear City Center, AZ
Santa Theresa International Project

Commercial Office Buildings
Eastland Tower, CA
Taco Bell Corporate Headquarters, CA
Airport Towers, CA
Murdock Plaza, CA
Western Savings Building, AZ
Wells Fargo Building, CA
Two Chatham Center, PA

Aerospace
Hughes EDSG Complex, CA
Hughes Radar Systems Buildings, CA
JPL Engineering Support Building, CA

Computer Facilities
CSC Offices and INFONET Center, CA
First Interstate Bank Center, CA

Health Care
Kaiser Hospitals, CA
Bakersfield Memorial Hospital, CA
Kenneth Norris Cancer Hospital, CA
Estelle Doheny Eye Hospital, CA
Sierra Medical Center, TX

Collaborative Projects
1000 Wilshire, CA (Kohn Pedersen Fox)
550 S. Hope St., CA (Kohn Pedersen Fox)
Gateway Plaza, CA (Kisho Kurakawa)
777 Tower, CA (Cesar Pelli)
The Aventine, CA (Michael Graves)
Creative Artists Agency, CA (I.M. Pei)

Hotels
Disneyland Complex Planning Studies, CA
Palm Springs Country Club, CA
The Aventine Hyatt, CA

Museums
J. Paul Getty Museum, CA
Richard Nixon Presidential Archives, CA
Newport Harbor Art Museum, CA

BACKGROUND
Since its founding in 1951, Langdon Wilson has completed an extensive portfolio of projects representative of the diversity of its practice. With offices in Los Angeles and Newport Beach, California and Phoenix, Arizona, LW has committed its resources to providing each client with the planning, design and technical services necessary to achieve the goals and objectives of each project. Over the past decade, LW has completed projects exceeding $3 billion in construction value.

PHILOSOPHY
Architectural design is both a visual art and a technical evolution in the use of materials. Success in design demands the resolution of a diverse set of specific requirements expressed by each client and the physical attributes of each site. We take pride in our ability to listen carefully to our clients; gaining a precise understanding of their goals and objectives and translating them into aesthetically, functionally and financially successful projects.

THE TEAM
Langdon Wilson's staff of more than 135 persons have studied, lived and worked worldwide. This diversity of cultural heritage and professional experience is contributed to each LW project. LW emphasizes the importance of teamwork and communication between all members of the project team including the owner and the contractor.

CADD
Langdon Wilson has been in the forefront of applying CADD to the process of architectural project development. Utilizing CADD on every project allows fast-track project schedules, faster turnaround time on project documentation from phase to phase, greater accuracy and an increase in the productive and creative use of our architects' time.

QUALITY CONTROL
Langdon Wilson believes effective quality control is a process which must begin in the earliest stages of project development. LW's commitment to this process permits the evaluation of design concepts and details to assure they meet with the objectives established with the client at the start of the project.

COLLABORATION
Langdon Wilson has established an enviable reputation for delivering projects high in quality and predictable in cost and schedule, leading increasing numbers of developers to request that LW associate with internationally renowned firms for the technical development of their projects.

The Westin Maui

The Westin Kauai

Hyatt Regency Waikiki

Hyatt Regency Maui

Hyatt Regency Waikoloa

LAWTON & UMEMURA, ARCHITECTS, AIA, INC.

LAWTON & UMEMURA, ARCHITECTS, AIA, INC.

ESTABLISHED
1977

ADDRESS
Hemmeter Corporation
Building
No. 1 Capitol District
Honolulu, HI 96813

TELEPHONE
(808) 529 9700

FACSIMILE
(808) 529 9713

EXECUTIVE OFFICERS
Herbert T. Lawton
- President and CEO
Robert K. Umemura
- Exec. Vice President and COO
Paul Ma
- Vice President/Director of Design
Colin H. Shimokawa
- Vice President/Secretary
Byron T. Tsuruda
- Vice President/Treasurer

REGIONAL OFFICES
Laguna Niguel, CA
Coral Springs, FL

NO. OF EMPLOYEES
120

PROJECT TYPE
Destination Resort Hotels

PERSON TO CONTACT
Robert K. Umemura, AIA

R. Umemura & H. Lawton

COMPLETED PROJECTS
King's Village Shopping Complex -
Honolulu, HI
Hyatt Regency Waikiki - Honolulu, HI
Kona Inn Shopping Village - Kona, HI
Hyatt Regency Maui - Kaanapali, HI
Keauhou Kona Shopping Village - Kona, HI
Nailert Park Hotel - Bangkok, Thailand
Carter Presidential Library - Atlanta, GA
The Westin Maui - Kaanapali, HI
The Westin Kauai at Kauai Lagoons
- Lihue, HI
Hyatt Regency Waikoloa - Kona, HI
Hemmeter Corporation Building
- Honolulu, HI

CURRENT PROJECTS
Monarch Beach Resort - Laguna Niguel, CA
Sint Maarten Resort - Netherland Antilles,
Caribbean Islands
Carter Chapel - Atlanta, GA
Key Biscayne Resort - Key Biscayne, FL
State Office Tower - Honolulu, HI
Waterfront Row - Kona, HI

FUTURE PROJECT SITES
Tucson, AZ
Sunterra, CA
Mazatlan, Mexico
Gold Coast, Australia
Okinawa
St. Croix, U.S. Virgin Islands
Bermuda Islands
Phase IV Kalapaki Bay, HI

1

2

3

4

5

1. Orange County John Wayne Airport, Orange County, CA
2. E.R. Squibb & Sons Distribution Center, Irvine, CA
3. Burbank Gateway Center, Burbank, CA
4. Four Hutton Centre, Santa Ana, CA
5. State Compensation Insurance Fund, Sacramento, CA
6. CalMat Corporate Headquarters, Los Angeles, CA

6

LEASON POMEROY ASSOCIATES, INC.
Architecture Planning
Interior Design

ESTABLISHED DATE
1965

OFFICE LOCATIONS
44 Plaza Square
Orange, CA 92666
Telephone   (714) 639 5541

3780 Wilshire Blvd., Suite 300
Los Angeles, CA 90010
Telephone   (213) 738 7655

4350 La Jolla Village Drive
Suite 130
San Diego, CA 92122
Telephone   (619) 587 6665

1215 G Street
Sacramento, CA 95814
Telephone   (916) 443 0335

DIRECTORS
Leason F. Pomeroy III, FAIA
William H. Bigelow III, AIA
Terry D. Jacobson, AIA
Robert O. Kupper, AIA
Dan Heinfeld, AIA
Philip L. Kroeze, AIA

NUMBER OF EMPLOYEES
150

PROJECT TYPES
Commercial
Corporate
Institutional
Educational
Retail
Mixed Use
Hospitality
Industrial/R&D

CURRENT AND RECENT PROJECTS

Commercial Office
State Compensation Insurance Fund, Sacramento, CA
Renaissance Center Office Park, Las Vegas, NV
4 Hutton Centre, Santa Ana, CA
Marina Village, Alameda, CA

Corporate
CalMat Corporate Headquarters, Los Angeles, CA
The Vons Companies, Inc., Headquarters, Arcadia, CA
AST Research Corporate Headquarters, Irvine, CA
IBM National Marketing Center, Southlake, TX

Institutional
Yuba City Hall, Yuba City, CA
North County Courthouse, Escondido, CA
Orange County John Wayne Airport, Orange County, CA

Educational
University Montessori Pre-School, Irvine, CA
Harold Hutton Sports Center, Orange, CA
UCI Campus Planning, Irvine, CA
UCLA Northwest Campus International Center, Los Angeles, CA
University of Arizona, Graduate School of Business, Planning, Tucson, AZ

Retail
Tustin Market Place, Tustin, CA
Burbank Gateway Center, Burbank, CA
River Center, Tucson, AZ
Wiltern Village, Los Angeles, CA

Hospitality
Marriott Hotel, Westlake, TX
Hyatt Regency Hotel, Los Angeles, CA

Industrial/R&D
E.R. Squibb & Sons Regional Distribution Center, Irvine, CA
Sanyo Distribution Center, San Diego, CA
Sherwood Medical, San Diego, CA
Home Savings of America, City of Industry, CA
Irvine Spectrum, Irvine, CA

BACKGROUND

Leason Pomeroy Associates, Inc. is experienced in the design and management of major mixed-use complexes, commercial office projects, specialty retail centers, research/manufacturing facilities, institutional facilities and educational projects. Over the years, the firm and its principals have come to be recognized for their leadership in urban planning, building design and interior design.

Assisted by the latest computer-aided design technology, LPA serves clients ranging from large corporations and national developers to governmental agencies. LPA provides a full scope of architectural, planning and interior design services from early program development to final design documents and construction administration.

LPA is rated among the top 30 Architectural Firms in Engineering News Record's 1988 Top 500 Design Firms, in Interior Design's Top 100 Interior Design Giants nationwide.

In the past 23 years, LPA has won over 120 regional and national design awards. These encompass a wide variety of project types and have one thing in common, the support of each client to LPA's commitment to design excellence.

Providing its clients with the highest professional services, LPA's project teams are comprised of professionals from the architectural and interior design disciplines. This approach allows them to better serve their clients by bringing the combined expertise of design professionals to the project.

More that eighty percent of the firm's workload has resulted from continuing relationships with existing clients. This is the strongest recommendation any architectural firm can have. It indicates clients' satisfaction with the quality of design and services rendered.

Leason **Pomeroy** *Associates*

THE LUCKMAN PARTNERSHIP, INC.

THE LUCKMAN PARTNERSHIP, INC.

ESTABLISHED
1950

ADDRESS
9220 Sunset Boulevard
Los Angeles, CA 90069

TELEPHONE
(213) 274 7755

FACSIMILE
(213) 274 1724

PARTNERS
James M. Luckman, AIA
Richard A. McKnew, AIA
Michael J. O'Sullivan, AIA
Jack C. Spak, AIA
Frederick M. Yerou, AIA

ASSOCIATE PARTNER
Roger Chikhani, AIA

NUMBER OF EMPLOYEES
60

PROJECT TYPES
Commercial
Educational
Museums/Theaters
Recreational
Hotel/Residential
Industrial
Rehabilitation/Restoration

PERSONS TO CONTACT
Any Partner

FIRM PROFILE

The Luckman Partnership, inc. is an architectural and planning firm with an experienced staff of design professionals, providing services to clients across the country.

For five years, from 1968 to 1973, the firm was affiliated with the Ogden Development Corporation. Through this association, we gained invaluable insight into the concerns of the developer client, ranging from development feasibility and structuring to leasing and operations. We understand the needs of the developer and our role as a member of the project team. Above all we appreciate our client's desire for the day to day participation of a partner in the project; as a manager, architect and leader of the team in the all important areas of cost and schedule control.

In the years since its inception, The Luckman Partnership has successfully designed more than $6 billion of diverse structures including more than 100 million square feet of office space, dozens of hotels, industrial and research facilities, educational facilities, retail establishments, communications and data processing facilities, sports and recreational centers, and is the recipient of over 100 separate design awards.

In spite of the evolution of the firm over the years, we have never ceased to stress and adhere to our philosophy of **quality planning and design, within the budget and on time.**

CURRENT AND RECENT PROJECTS

Commercial
Business Arts Plaza
Cadillac Fairview Office Tower
Culver Studios Office Building
Oceangate Office Towers
Peterson Publishing International Headquarters
Prudential Western Regional Headquarters
Shamrock Center Office Buildings I and II
Warner Bros. Office Building
Wilshire Place Office Tower
Xerox Headquarters

Educational
Adelphi University Master Plan
Cal State Long Beach Engineering Building
Los Angeles Child Guidance Clinic

Fine Arts/Theater Facilities
Buffalo Bill Museum
Cal State Los Angeles Arts Complex
Oklahoma Christian College Special Events Center
Olmsted Theater Renovation, Adelphi University
Phoenix Symphony Hall

Recreational
Aloha Stadium
EPCOT Center - Land Pavilion
EPCOT Center - Imagination Pavilion
The Forum
Madison Square Garden
Orange County Convention Center
Phoenix Convention Center
Sullivan Arena

Hotels
Holiday Casino Las Vegas
Hyatt Regency Dearborn
Hyatt Regency Los Angeles
Hyatt Regency Phoenix

Rehabilitation/Restoration
California Federal Savings And Loan Headquarters
First Interstate Bank Tower
Pacific Bell Office Building

Master Plan, Mercy Hospital of Pittsburgh

Stage Entrance, Benedum Center for the Performing Arts

Porte Cochere, Mercy Hospital of Pittsburgh

Support Building, Benedum Center for the Performing Arts

MACLACHLAN, CORNELIUS & FILONI, ARCHITECTS, INC.

MACLACHLAN, CORNELIUS & FILONI, ARCHITECTS, INC.
Architects, Planners and Designers

ESTABLISHED
1889

ADDRESS
200 The Bank Tower
Pittsburgh, PA 15222

TELEPHONE
(412) 281 6568

OFFICERS
Clare C. Cornelius, AIA
Albert L. Filoni, AIA
Kenneth K. Lee, AIA
David A. Lowry, AIA

DIRECTORS
Joseph W. Carlson, Jr., R.A.
Robert H. Holt, Jr., R.A.
Richard E. Schmitz, R.A.

PROJECT TYPES AND DISCIPLINES
Planning, Programming, Architecture, and Interiors for New Construction Renovation and Historic Restoration, Civic, Educational, Theater Arts, Health Care, Institutional, Liturgical, and Residential Environments.

CURRENT AND RECENT PROJECTS

Health Care
The Mercy Hospital of Pittsburgh, PA
- Master Plans I and II
- Tower and Service Extension
- Heliport
Sewickley Valley Hospital, PA
- South Wing Expansion
- Medical Office Building
Renovations to:
Suburban General Hospital, Pittsburgh, PA
Braddock General Hospital, PA

Performance Facilities
The Pittsburgh Trust for Cultural Resources, PA
- Benedum Center for the Performing Arts
- Fulton Theater Study
Pittsburgh Symphony Society, PA
- Heinz Hall for the Performing Arts and Garden Plaza
D & E Management Company, Harrison City, PA
- Outdoor Amphitheater
Coyle Theater, Charleroi, PA
Washington and Jefferson College, PA
- Olin Fine Arts Center

Proscenium, Benedum Center

California University of Pennsylvania
- Steele Auditorium
Indiana University of Pennsylvania
- Waller Hall/Theater by the Grove
Duquesne University, Pittsburgh, PA
- Performing Arts Center
Hartwood Acres, Allegheny County, PA
- Performing Stage and Support Building

Educational
Denison University, OH
- Master Plan - Swasey Chapel
  - Colwell House
- Science Technology Building
Washington & Jefferson College, PA
- Master Plan - Residence Hall
  - Campus Center
- Business Classroom Building
- Dieter Porter Life Science Building
Indiana University of Pennsylvania
- Breezedale Alumni House
Bethany College, Bethany, WV
- Grace Phillips Johnson Visual Arts Center
- Harder Hall Leadership Center
- Health & Recreational Complex

Residential
Brodhead House - Ligonier, PA
Eichleay House - Ligonier, PA
Hunt Stable Residences - Ligonier, PA

Commercial/Business
Forbes Trail Development Co.
- Waterfront Commercial Office Building, Pittsburgh, PA
Landmark Savings Association
- Clearview Branch, Pittsburgh, PA
Eat'n Park Restaurants, Inc., Pittsburgh, PA
Heinz U.S.A., Pittsburgh, PA
- Administrative Offices Planning
Developments Inc.
- Physicians Office Building, Pittsburgh, PA
Heinz Family Offices, Pittsburgh, PA

Liturgical
Renovations to:
Shadyside Presbyterian Church, Pittsburgh, PA
St. Paul's Episcopal Church, Pittsburgh, PA
Bethany Memorial Church, Bethany, WV
Bellaire Christian Church, Bellaire, OH
Additions and Alterations to:
Christian Church of Pennsylvania/ Laurelview

St. Catherine of Sweden Parish, Wildwood, PA
St. Regis Church, Trafford, PA
First Christian Church of Canonsburg, PA
First Presbyterian Church of California, PA
The Mercy Hospital of Johnstown, PA Chapel

Civic
City of Pittsburgh, PA - River Safety Center
Womansplace, Pittsburgh, PA
Allegheny County Cultural Alliance, Pittsburgh, PA - TIX Booth
Laughlin Children's Center, Sewickley, PA

Recreational
Rolling Rock Club, Ligonier, PA
- Renovations
Longue Vue Club, Verona, PA - Master Plan
Kennywood Park, West Mifflin, PA
- The Pagoda

HISTORY
MacLachlan, Cornelius & Filoni, Inc., is the continuing successor to the firm founded in 1889 by Edward Stotz. Throughout our organization's long history, we have maintained a wide diversity in architectural practice, having programmed, designed, and supervised the construction of all types of buildings. In particular, our firm has earned wide respect for knowledge of health care facilities, centers for the performing arts, business/commercial buildings, and for abilities in the fields of historical restoration and rehabilitation.

Years of experience and familiarity with current problem-solving techniques and building methods enable us to meet any challenge in the field of Architectural planning, design, engineering, or the construction process.

We are a very personable organization. The principals are directly involved in all aspects of the work from beginning to end. While we always strive for excellence in design, our goal of problem-free building performance tempers our work with a common-sense perspective.

Our many repeat clients attest to the fact that no project is too large or too small for us to consider. MacLachlan, Cornelius & Filoni, Inc. designs for people. Working directly with the client, our team of professionals helps define the goals, directions and guidelines that assure the client's functional, aesthetic and budget requirements are satisfied.

Admissions Offices, Mercy Hospital

1

2

1. Village "C" Student Housing,
   Georgetown University
2. International Medical Center of Rabat, Morocco
3. Healy Hall Renovation and Restoration,
   Georgetown University
4. U.S. International Cultural and Trade Center,
   Washington, DC
5. National Rehabilitation Hospital, Washington, DC

3

4

5

MARIANI & ASSOCIATES

MARIANI & ASSOCIATES
Architects Planners Engineers

ESTABLISHED DATE
1957

ADDRESS
1600 20th Street, N.W.
Washington, DC 20009

TELEPHONE
(202) 462 5656

FACSIMILE
(202) 462 7249

DIRECTORS
Theodore F. Mariani, FAIA
Reginald H. Cude, AIA

NUMBER OF EMPLOYEES
34

PROJECT TYPES
Health Care
Educational
Institutional
Historic Preservation

OTHER DISCIPLINES
Interior Design
Space Planning
Master Planning
Cost Estimating

PERSON TO CONTACT
Theodore F. Mariani, FAIA
Reginald H. Cude, AIA

CURRENT & RECENT PROJECTS

Educational
Thomas & Dorothy Leavey Center, Georgetown University, Washington, DC. Construction Cost $35m.

Village "C" Student Housing, Georgetown University, Washington, DC. Construction Cost $16m.

Student Union II Addition, George Mason University, Fairfax, VA. Construction Cost $2.2m.

Health Care
National Rehabilitation Hospital, Washington, DC. Construction Cost $20m.

International Medical Center of Rabat, Rabat, Morocco. Construction Cost $30m.

Fort Washington Community Hospital Addition, Prince Georges County, MD. Construction Cost $2.2m.

Children's Rehabilitation Center Addition, University of Virginia, Charlottesville, VA. Construction Cost $2.6m.

Master Planning/Programming/Consulting
U.S. International Cultural & Trade Center, Washington, DC. Construction Cost $385m.

Capital Point Redevelopment, Washington, DC. Construction Cost $200m.

Mount Vernon Square Development, Washington, DC. Construction Cost $170m.

South Campus Development, Mount Saint Mary's College, Emmitsburg, MD. Construction Cost $9m.

Rusk Institute of N.Y.U. Medical Center, New York, NY. Construction Cost $50m.

Commercial/Office
Cherry Hill Construction Co. Headquarters, Laurel, MD. Construction Cost $2.4m.

G.B.A. Office Building, Fairfax, VA. Construction Cost $20m.

Interiors/Space Planning
U.S. Forest Service Offices, Washington, DC. Construction Cost $5m.

American Management Systems Offices, New York, NY. Construction Cost $.3m.

Historic Preservation/Adaptive Reuse
Old Cabell Hall Restoration, University of Virginia, Charlottesville, VA. Construction Cost $2.1m.

Auditors Building Renovation, Washington, DC. Construction Cost $18m.

Historic Structure Preservation Guides, Cape Hatteras National Seashore, NC, Carl Sandburg Home National Historic Site, NC. Construction Cost N/A.

Survey of Historically Significant Housing Quarters, U.S. Army/Nationwide. Construction Cost N/A.

AWARDS

Design Award
The Masonry Institute,
Village "C" Student Housing,
Georgetown University.

Award for Achievement of Excellence in Architecture
Washington Chapter, AIA,
Nevils East Campus Housing,
Georgetown University.

Award for Distinctive Residential Architecture
Washingtonian/AIA Residential Awards Program,
Nevils East Campus Housing,
Georgetown University.

Award of Excellence
Middle Atlantic Region, AIA,
WMATA Montgomery Division Metrobus Garage.

Award of Excellence
Middle Atlantic Region, AIA,
Healy Hall Stair Addition,
Georgetown University.

Award For Achievement of Excellence in Architecture
Washington Chapter, AIA,
WMATA Montgomery Division Metrobus Garage.

Merit Award for Achievement of Excellence in Historic Preservation and Architecture
Washington Chapter, AIA,
Healy Hall Stair Addition,
Georgetown University.

Citation for Achievement of Excellence In Historic Preservation and Architecture
Washington Chapter, AIA,
PEPCO Georgetown Substation.

Award
Montgomery County Planning Board,
Maryland National Capital Park and Planning Commission,
Potomac Meadows Housing Design Competition.

Merit Award for Excellence in Architecture
Potomac Valley Chapter, AIA,
Parking Structure,
Georgetown University Medical Center.

PROFILE
Mariani & Associates is known for innovative design solutions to a wide variety of architectural and planning problems. The firm has produced distinctive, award-winning buildings while solving difficult problems on a diverse range of Educational, Medical, Commercial, Industrial, and Residential Projects. We serve both public and private sector clients, domestic as well as international, and handle work ranging from master plans for large multi-building developments to the smallest individual structures. Our aim is always to produce the best possible building within the constraints of the Owner's budget, site, and schedule. We employ a studio system, with each project being assigned to a specific team which follows that project through from inception to occupancy. We believe our numerous repeat clients and the expanding scope of our projects is the best testimony to the validity of our approach to architectural practice.

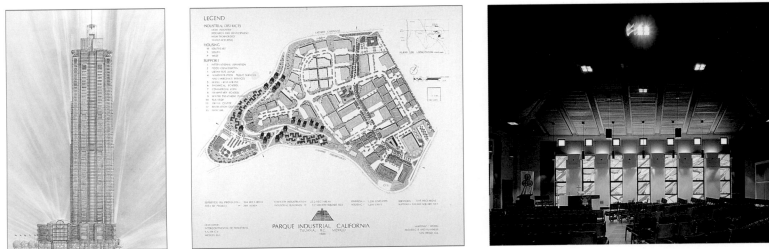

MARTINEZ/WONG & ASSOCIATES, INC.

J. Martinez   J.O. Wong

MARTINEZ/WONG & ASSOCIATES, INC.
Architecture Planning Interiors
Urban Design

ESTABLISHED
1980

ADDRESS
701 "B" Street
Imperial Bank Tower
Suite 440
San Diego, CA 92101

TELEPHONE
(619) 233 4857

FACSIMILE
(619) 237 0541

DIRECTORS
Joseph Martinez, AIA
Joseph O. Wong, AIA

NUMBER OF EMPLOYEES
28

PROJECT TYPES
Commercial
Educational
Governmental
Health
Hotel/Resort
Industrial
Mixed-Use
Residential
Specialty Boutiques

OTHER DISCIPLINES
Geographic Information
Systems
Interiors
Planning
Urban Design

PERSON TO CONTACT
Joseph Martinez
Joseph O. Wong

CURRENT AND RECENT PROJECTS

Waterfront Developments
Harbor Center San Diego/Solar Industries
One Port Plaza, San Diego Embarcadero
"G" Street Mole National Design
Competition, San Diego
Strand Master Plan, Oceanside, CA

Hotels and Resorts
Doubletree Hotel, Mission Valley, San Diego
Best Western, Rancho Bernardo
Radisson Suites Hotel, San Diego
Hilton Hotel, Del Mar, CA
Trusthouse Forte, Long Beach, CA
Hotel-by-the-Sea, Carlsbad
Kearny Mesa Holiday Inn, San Diego
Hotel Palmilla, Mexico

Mixed-Use Centers
Prospect Point, La Jolla
Le Jardin, La Jolla
Kaohsiung Hotel/Mixed-Use Centre
Broadway Towne Center, Chula Vista
Fifth and Laurel Center, San Diego
Park Square, Chula Vista
Hippo-Citron, La Jolla

Governmental/Institutional
Lindo Lake Town Hall, Lakeside, CA
Blinder Multi-Purpose Center, Oceanside
North Island Naval Station Master Plan
The Career Center, University of California,
San Diego
The Joslyn Nutrition Center, City of
Escondido
Children's Museum of San Diego, La Jolla
Village Square
Fire Station 24, Del Mar

Office Centers
LAX International Center, Los Angeles
Cheng Financial, San Diego
Williams Office Centre, Riverside
Alhambra Center, Los Angeles
One Olympic Tower, Los Angeles

Industrial Research and Development
Parque Industrial California, Tijuana,
B.C. Mexico
Jerome's Furniture Distribution Center,
San Diego
Complex B, Rancho California

Housing
Martinez/Wong have designed over 5,000
units of housing during the past six years,
including luxury condominium towers,
single family tracts, multi-family
condominiums, apartments, senior housing,
congregate care, as well as, custom
residences.

APPROACH TO THE ENVIRONMENT
We view the natural and built environment
as a delicate entity with its own history,
culture, and future. The architects, planners
and urban designers at Martinez/Wong
follow the lead established by the principal
designers in developing each project as a
unique place which is beautiful and vital to
its context.

It has been our nature to approach each
project in a team effort consisting of the
client, the users, and the architect; and,
within a studio atmosphere at our office, the
principal, project architect(s), and assigned
staff start and complete the project together.

CORPORATE PROFILE
Martinez/Wong is an interdisciplinary firm
engaged in the practice of architecture,
planning, interiors and urban design. Since
our inception, we have designed over 400
projects with a construction value in excess
of $1.2 billion dollars. The firm was
established in 1980 by Joseph Martinez and
Joseph O. Wong.

Mr. Martinez received his Master of
Architecture degree from Harvard
University in 1975 and his Bachelor of Arts
from the University of California, San Diego
in 1971. In 1987, he was named a
"Centennial Alumnus" by the National
Association of Colleges and Universities.
He is a corporate member of the American
Institute of Architects and actively involved
in many community organizations as well as
teaching architecture and urban design at
the University of California, San Diego.

Mr. Wong received his Master of
Architecture and Bachelor of Arts degrees
from the University of California, Berkeley;
and, his Master of Landscape Architecture
degree from Harvard University in 1975.
Mr. Wong is a corporate member of the
American Institute of Architects and is
involved in several civic organizations,
including the Public Arts Advisory Board.

Martinez/Wong is the recipient of 21 design
awards and prizes in local, regional and
national competitions, including honors
from the American Institute of Architects
and the American Planning Association.

Accordingly, we are interested in producing
good design which celebrates the activities
of place and space.

1

2

4

5

1. Kris Kelly, San Francisco, CA
2. Dai-Ichi Hotel Tokyo Bay, Tokyo, Japan
3. Queen Street Building, Honolulu, HI
4. Hotel Hana-Maui, Hana, HI
5. Sheraton Fiji, Nadi, Fiji
6. Susan Marie, Honolulu, HI
7. Logos (clockwise from top left):
   City of Kapolei, HI
   Capitol District, Honolulu, HI
   Ala Moana Hotel, Honolulu, HI

6

7

(L-R): Bon-Hui Uy, Melvyn Choy, Evan Cruthers, Michael Leineweber and Peter Caderas

MEDIA FIVE LIMITED
A Design Corporation

ESTABLISHED DATE
1972

ADDRESS
345 Queen Street, 2nd Floor
Honolulu, HI 96813

TELEPHONE
(808) 524 2040

FACSIMILE
(808) 538 1529

TELEX
MEDIA 7431380

PRINCIPALS
Evan D. Cruthers, AIA
Melvyn Y.K. Choy, AIA, RAIA
Bon-Hui Uy
Michael J. Leineweber, AIA
Peter Caderas
Hideo Murakami

NUMBER OF EMPLOYEES
65

DISCIPLINES
Architecture
Graphic Design
Interior Design
Planning
Programming

PERSON TO CONTACT
Evan D. Cruthers, AIA

SELECTED CURRENT AND RECENT PROJECTS

Resorts
Hope Island Resort, Gold Coast, Australia
Hotel Hana-Maui renovation, Hana, HI
LeLagon Pacific Resort, Port Vila, Vanuatu
Hotel Nikko Guam interiors, Tumon Bay, Guam
Palau Pacific Resort, Arakabesan Island, Republic of Belau
Sheraton Fiji, Nadi, Fiji
Sheraton Kauai renovation, Poipu Beach, HI

Hotels
Ala Moana Hotel renovation, Honolulu, HI
Breezbay Hotel interiors, Yokohama, Japan
Dai-Ichi Hotel Tokyo Bay interiors, Tokyo, Japan
Hotel New Grand Saison Yokohama interiors, Yokohama, Japan
Manhatten Hotel interiors, Tokyo, Japan
New Otani Kaimana Beach Hotel renovation, Honolulu, HI
Palace on the Hill, Naha, Okinawa, Japan

Office Buildings
Gentry Pacific Center renovation, Honolulu, HI
Mahukona Office Building, Honolulu, HI
OCT Ocean View Center, Honolulu, HI
One Waterfront Plaza, Honolulu, HI

Corporate Offices
Kobayashi, Watanabe, Sugita, Kawashima & Goda, Honolulu, HI
Menke, Fahrney & Carroll, Costa Mesa, CA
Outrigger Hotels Hawaii, Honolulu, HI

Health Care Facilities
Fronk Clinics at Honolulu and Aiea, HI
Kahi Mohala Psychiatric Hospital renovation, Honolulu, HI
Pali Momi Medical Center interiors, Aiea, HI
Straub Family Health Centers at Kaneohe, Kailua and Mililani, HI

Industrial and Technical Facilities
Honolulu International Airport new concourses, Honolulu, HI
Gas Express Stations, Honolulu, HI
University of Hawaii at Hilo Research and Technology Center, Hilo, HI

Recreational Facilities
Naniloa Hotel Spa, Hilo, HI
Sanaru-ko Suburban Sports Club and Hotel, Hamamatsu, Japan
Sun Hills Country Club, Utsunomiya, Japan
Tokyu 700 Club, Chiba Prefecture, Japan

Residential
Mauna Lani Point Condominiums, Kohala Coast, HI
Prestige Condominiums, Tokyo, Japan
University of Hawaii at Hilo Student Housing, Hilo, HI

Shopping Complexes
Ala Moana Plaza, Honolulu, HI
The Pavilion and Colonnade at Ward Centre, Honolulu, HI
Kahala Mall additions, Honolulu, HI
Rainbow Bazaar renovation, Hilton Hawaiian Village, Honolulu, HI

Retail
Kris Kelly Linen Shop, San Francisco, CA
Summerhill, Colonnade at Ward Centre, Honolulu, HI
Susan Marie, Hawaii and California
W.H. Smith Resort shops, Wailea, Hawaii and Indian Wells, CA

Restaurants
Cafe Intra and Ristorante Attore, Hotel Seiyo Ginza, Tokyo, Japan
Chez Sushi and Big Ed's, Colonnade at Ward Centre, Honolulu, HI
Keo's, Il Fresco and Compadres, Pavilion at Ward Centre, Honolulu, HI
Kyoto Restaurants, Kyoto Royal Hotel, Kyoto, Japan

PROFILE OF MEDIA FIVE
At Media Five, design is a total concept. For this reason, we engage in its total scope, offering a combination of services in architecture, graphic design, interior design, planning and programming. These services are provided separately, in combination or comprehensively, according to our clients' need for a strong, well-integrated project identity.

We have designed a wide range of hotel/resort, recreational, medical, commercial, residential and industrial/technical facilities for private sector and government clients in Hawaii, California, Mexico, Canada, Australia and the Pacific Island nations, Japan, Korea, China and the British Indian Ocean Territories. And whether it is a destination resort, a restaurant or a corporate office, every project is carefully designed to make an essential statement -- one that is appropriate, special, and above all, personal.

Since 1972, Media Five has evolved and grown according to a certain aspiration: to be the Pacific Basin's center for design. We have been building toward this goal on the strength of superior performance, both contractual and creative, the talent of our people, the teamwork we inspire, and the trust we have won in the business of design.

RICHARD MEIER & PARTNERS

Richard Meier

RICHARD MEIER & PARTNERS

PARTNERS
Richard Meier, FAIA
Donald Barker, AIA
Robert F. Gatje, FAIA
Michael Palladino, AIA
Thomas Phifer, AIA

ADDRESS
475 Tenth Avenue
New York, NY 10018

TELEPHONE
(212) 967 6060

FACSIMILE
(212) 967 3207

SELECTED CURRENT AND RECENT PROJECTS

Museum of Contemporary Art,
Barcelona, Spain

Masterplan,
Maybury Office Park,
Edinburgh, Scotland

Research and Laboratory Facilities,
Daimler-Benz
Ulm, Federal Republic of Germany

Masterplan,
Administrative and Maritime Center,
Antwerp, Belgium

Corporate Headquarters,
Canal +
Paris, France

Corporate Headquarters,
Royal Dutch Paper Mills,
Hilversum, The Netherlands

Exhibition, Training and Dining Facilities,
Max Weishaupt GmBH,
Schwendi, Federal Republic of Germany

Alumni and Admissions Center,
Cornell University,
Ithaca, NY

City Hall and Central Library,
The Hague, The Netherlands

Exhibition and Assembly Building,
Ulm, Federal Republic of Germany

Eye Center,
Oregon Health Sciences University,
Portland, OR

J. Paul Getty Center,
Los Angeles, CA

Bridgeport Center,
Bridgeport, CT

Office and Laboratory Complex,
Siemens AG,
Munich, Federal Republic of Germany

Des Moines Art Center Addition,
Des Moines, IA

The High Museum of Art,
Atlanta, GA

Museum for Decorative Arts,
Frankfurt, Federal Republic of Germany

Hartford Seminary,
Hartford, CT

The Atheneum,
New Harmony, IN

Bronx Developmental Center,
Bronx, NY

FIRM BACKGROUND
Since the firm's founding in 1963, its work has included museum and other cultural institutions, offices, schools, medical facilities, housing and private residences. Its completed projects range in size from 1,000 to over 1,000,000 square feet. Despite the variety of its work, the firm remains committed to excellent design and unsparingly high quality and has won numerous design awards and public recognition. Each project, regardless of size, is given the same meticulous attention. To achieve this, Richard Meier is personally responsible for all phases of each project, from analysis and design through detailing and construction, with his partners assuring expert day-to-day management.

SELECTED AWARDS
Royal Gold Medal,
Royal Institute of British Architects

Pritzker Architecture Prize

Arnold Brunner Memorial Prize, American Academy and Institute of Arts and Letters

Medal of Honor,
American Institute of Architects,
New York Chapter

American Institute of Architects Honor Awards:
Museum for Decorative Arts
High Museum of Art
The Atheneum
Hartford Seminary
Bronx Developmental Center
Westbeth Artists' Housing
Twin Parks Northeast Housing
Douglas House
Smith House

1

2

1. AB Volvo Corporate Headquarters
   Photographer Credit: Keld Helmer-Petersen
2. IBM Customer Executive Education Center
   Photographer Credit: Jock Pottle
3. RPI Center for Industrial Innovation
   Photographer Credit: Paul Warchol
4. Hampton Roads History Center/VA Air & Space Center
   Photographer Credit: Jock Pottle

3

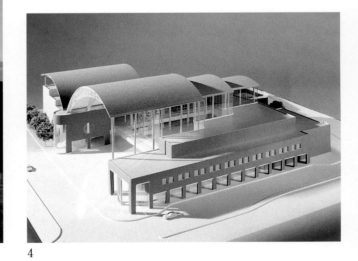

4

MITCHELL/GIURGOLA ARCHITECTS NEW YORK

MITCHELL/GIURGOLA ARCHITECTS NEW YORK

ESTABLISHED DATE
1958; 1986

ADDRESS
170 West 97th Street
New York, NY 10025

TELEPHONE
(212) 663 4000

FACSIMILE
(212) 866 5006

PARTNERS
Romaldo Giurgola, FAIA, FRAIA
Paul Broches, AIA
Steven M. Goldberg, AIA
Jan Keane, AIA
John M. Kurtz, AIA
Randy Leach, AIA
Mark J. Markiewicz, AIA
Dart Sageser, AIA

NUMBER OF EMPLOYEES
30

PROJECT TYPES

Corporate/Commercial
Headquarters, Offices, Retail,
Conference Facilities, Parking,
Industrial Parks

Cultural Centers/Libraries
Museums, Concert Halls, Theaters,
Libraries

Educational
Campus Master Planning,
Classrooms, Laboratories,
Libraries, Dormitories, Athletic
Facilities

Government
Offices, Courtrooms

Laboratory/Health
Biological and Industrial Research
Laboratories, Health Care Centers

Residential
Apartment Towers, Residences,
Housing Developments

OTHER DISCIPLINES
Urban Design and Master Planning
Interior Design
Space Planning

PERSON TO CONTACT
Steven M. Goldberg

CURRENT AND RECENT PROJECTS

Corporate/Commercial
AB Volvo Corporate Headquarters,
Goteborg, Sweden*
IBM Customer Executive Education Center,
Palisades, NY
IBM Office Park, Westlake/Southlake, TX*
Center West Office Tower, Los Angeles*
300 Atlantic Street Office Complex,
Stamford, CT
Parking/Retail Facility, Hampton, VA*

Cultural Centers/Libraries
Anchorage Historical & Fine Arts
Museum, AK*
Hampton Roads History Center/VA
Air & Space Center, Hampton, VA*
Fine & Performing Arts Center, University of
West Florida, Pensacola*
Johnson County Central Library, Overland
Park, KS*

Government
New Parliament House, Canberra, Australia
(Mitchell/Giurgola & Thorp)
Wainwright Office Complex, St. Louis, MO*

Laboratory/Health
Health Services and Whitaker College of
Health Sciences, Technology and
Management, MIT, Cambridge*
Center for Industrial Innovation,
RPI, Troy, NY
Outpatient Care Center, UCLA*
Emerging Technologies Complex,
University of Vermont, Burlington
Revelle Sciences Building, UCSD*
Life Sciences Laboratory, Ciba-Geigy
Corporation, Summit, NJ
Science Laboratory, College of Staten Island,
City University of New York
Ceramics Corridor Projects, Alfred
Technology Resources, Inc., Corning
and Alfred, NY

Planning
Master Plan, IBM and Maguire/Thomas
Partners, Westlake/Southlake, TX*
Master Plan, IBM Customer Executive
Education Center, Palisades, NY

Residential
Residential Development, White Plains, NY
Hudson View East Residential
Development, Battery Park City, NYC
*In association with local firm.

DESIGN PHILOSOPHY
Mitchell/Giurgola Architects is committed
to the search for an architecture capable of
enriching life and of providing a sense of
inspiration and engagement to its
inhabitants. Each building derives its form
from a specific architectural response to its
programmatic intent, site, environmental
conditions, and dialogue with its patrons.

The practice has been characterized by a
constant commitment to an architecture
based on humanistic principles, balanced by
a search for life-enhancing solutions to built
forms; the ultimate resolution of the form
maintains a level of independence and
presence that is unique to itself. It is the
tension between these seemingly
contradictory qualities that is the genesis of
our search for architectural form.

The firm has developed and consistently
embraces a design methodology that
revolves around design teams formed at the
outset of each project. This approach
provides a fresh solution to each client's
project. Equally important is the continuity
of each architectural team from the early
design phases through construction
administration, thereby ensuring a
consistent attitude toward conceptual issues
and technical matters.

HISTORY
Mitchell/Giurgola Architects was founded
in Philadelphia as a partnership between
Ehrman B. Mitchell Jr. and Romaldo
Giurgola in 1958, and, in 1968, opened an
office in New York.

In 1976 the firm received the Firm Award of
the American Institute of Architects, the
highest award that the Institute can bestow
upon a practicing group. Romaldo Giurgola
was awarded the Institute's 1982 Gold
Medal for his leadership in design. Ehrman
B. Mitchell Jr. (FAIA) served as President of
the national AIA from 1978-1980 and retired
from the firm in 1984.

Mitchell/Giurgola Architects New York was
formed in 1986 and continues to provide the
same high standard of professionalism with
a stable senior leadership that is unchanged
since the early 1970's. A tightly knit
working method and design philosophy has
resulted from limiting the size of the firm
and by having substantial participation in all
projects by the principals.

Murphy/Jahn

MURPHY/JAHN

MURPHY/JAHN
Helmut Jahn

Helmut Jahn, President and Chief Executive Officer, has earned a reputation on the cutting edge of progressive architecture in the 1970's and 1980's. His buildings have had a "staggering" influence on world architecture according to John Zukowsky, Curator of Architecture at the Art Institute of Chicago. Murphy/Jahn's buildings have received numerous design awards and have been represented in architectural exhibitions around the world.

OFFICES
Main Office
Murphy/Jahn, Inc.
35 E. Wacker Drive
Chicago, IL 60601
Telephone (312) 427 7300
Facsimile   (312) 332 0274

New York
Murphy/Jahn Architects, P.C.
535 Madison Avenue
New York, NY 10022
Telephone (212) 486 7666
Facsimile   (212) 486 0752

Frankfurt
Murphy/Jahn Architects, Inc.
Ludwig-Erhard-Anlage 1
D6000 Frankfurt 1
Telephone 011 49 69 756 1090
Facsimile   011 49 69 745 692

CORPORATE OFFICERS

Helmut Jahn
Sam Scaccia
Philip Castillo
Robert Goldberg
Brian O'Connor
Scott Pratt
Rainer Schildknecht
Martin F. Wolf
Nadezda Andric
Art Herbstman
William T. Lohmann
Keith H. Palmer
Dennis Recek
Ed Wilkas

OVERVIEW

Murphy/Jahn is a unique architectural firm conceived to meet the challenges posed by the 1990's and beyond. Under the leadership of Helmut Jahn, the practice has grown and evolved steadily from the original firm which was founded over 50 years ago. Through 20 years of "organization building" Murphy/Jahn has succeeded in combining the best of **Design Creativity** and **Corporate Professionalism**. We believe our commitment to this balance is fundamental to the successful translation from architectural concept into built reality. We are committed to creating forward reaching buildings which will endure the test of time and become a source of pride in the minds of owners, users, communities, and ourselves.

PEOPLE

The choice of an architect is ultimately a personal decision based upon professional trust vested in the principals, key employees, and staff of the architectural firm. Our staff of 150 includes the creative talents of architects, planners, interior designers, specifications writers, and business support personnel. We pride ourselves on a solid record of performance in delivering architectural service in a manner consistent with each client's pragmatic concerns. All key individuals in our firm are sensitive to the importance of the client's pragmatic concerns, and we further understand that the continued success of our firm depends on our record of client satisfaction.

DESIGN APPROACH/PHILOSOPHY

The Murphy/Jahn approach to design is both rational and intuitive; it attempts to give each building its own philosophical and intellectual base and establishes an opportunity to exploit its particular elements to achieve a visual and communicative statement. The rational part deals with the realities of a problem. The intuitive aspect deals with the theoretical, intellectual aspects - - a subconscious ability to sense the intrinsic structure of a problem and establish priorities for the elements of design which deal with space, form, light, color and materials and the way architecture communicates through symbol and meaning of architectural language.

PRACTICE PROFILE

We maintain a highly diversified practice serving a broad spectrum of private, corporate, institutional and governmental clients. While the general public has come to know Murphy/Jahn primarily through exposure to our largest highrise and commercial structures in publications like Time, Newsweek, Business Week, and Forbes, our practice is by no means limited to these project types. The diversity of our work, stimulates a cross fertilization of ideas and an intellectual freshness derived from addressing and resolving new architectural challenges. In order to succeed with this endeavor, we have established a policy that each commission will receive the full attention of Helmut Jahn.

PROJECT PROFILES

United Airlines Terminal

"Murphy/Jahn has given United one of the most extraordinary terminals in the nation. The architect has devised an inventive and efficient solution to the problem of moving passengers from the terminal to their planes, creating an animated flow of people through well-integrated, wonderfully detailed spaces."   - The Chicago Tribune, Paul Gapp

"If you haven't been to the United Airlines new terminal in Chicago, look forward to it. What a total difference a few more bucks for first-rate architecture make to everyone and everything it impacts."   - Forbes

"The United Terminal does not look back literally, of course - this is a building rich in the technological advances of our time. The O'Hare Terminal is the most impressive work of airport architecture since Eero Saarinen's Dulles Airport."
          - The New York Times, Paul Goldberger

State of Illinois Center

"Breathtaking spectacular inside, where its atrium does a noise thumbing job at practically everything except St. Peter's."   - Chicago Tribune, Paul Gapp

"The center, occupying an entire downtown block, is in a word, spectacular."
          - Los Angeles Times, Sam Hall Kaplan

One Liberty Place

"Not only far and away the best tall building that has been built in Philadelphia in more than 50 years - surely the finest skyscraper this city has seen since 1932."   - The New York Times, Paul Goldberger

"A visible bursting-out of energy in a city that had lagged during the national office boom of the 1980's."   - Philadelphia Inquirer, Thomas Hine

Chicago Board of Trade Addition

"Beyond doubt, this sky lobby lined with traders offices, is the most spectacular new space in town, a dazzler affixed to a landmark skyscraper that dominates the financial district."
          - Chicago Sun-Times, M.W. Newman

Park Avenue Tower

"By far the most flamboyant and commercially successful architect of his generation, Jahn is watching his imaginative high-rises shoot up in cities throughout the U.S. and Europe. And he knows how to give a client what he wants."
          - Fortune, Brian Dumaine

Northwestern Atrium Center

"It stamps Jahn irrefutably as the city's preeminent designer of spectacular public interiors that have revived the art of civic monumentality. Jahn is still the unchallenged master of the big space in Chicago, and Northwestern Center is surely among his best American Buildings."
          - Chicago Tribune, Paul Gapp

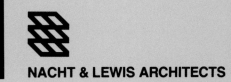

NACHT & LEWIS ARCHITECTS

NACHT & LEWIS ARCHITECTS

Directors (L-R): R. Lewis, R. Nelson, D. Keith and R. Carter

NACHT & LEWIS ARCHITECTS, INC.

ESTABLISHED
1922

ADDRESSES

Sacramento
7300 Folsom Boulevard, Suite 200
Sacramento, CA 95826
Telephone (916) 381 0127
Facsimile (916) 381 0310

Marina Del Rey
330 Washington Street, Suite 309
Marina Del Rey, CA 90292
Telephone (213) 306 9561

DIRECTORS
Richard L. Lewis, FAIA
- President
Denis Keith, AIA
- Vice President
Robert A. Nelson, AIA
- Vice President
Robert L. Carter, AIA
- Vice President

NUMBER OF EMPLOYEES
62

PROJECT TYPES
Commercial
Educational
Health Care
Interior Design
Governmental
- Federal, State, County & City

PERSON TO CONTACT
Richard L. Lewis, FAIA
Robert L. Carter, AIA

CURRENT AND RECENT PROJECTS

Commercial
A&E Investment Office,
Sacramento, CA $2.5m.
World Savings Plaza,
Sacramento, CA $2.5m.
Sunrise Plaza Hotel/Retail Center,
Los Angeles, CA $18.0m.

Educational
School of Business and Public
Administration, CSU, Sacramento $7.5m.
Plumas Hall, CSU, Chico $8.5m.
Florin High School, Elk Grove Unified
School District $19.0m.
Bear Creek High School, Lodi Unified
School District $15.0m.
Merrill F. West High School, Tracy Joint
Union High School District $30.0m.

Health
Medical Office Building,
Kaiser Permanente, Davis, CA $4.0m.
Women's & Children's Center, Mercy
San Juan Hospital, Carmichael, CA $4.0m.
Master Plan, Remodel & Expansion
Projects, Mercy San Juan Hospital,
Carmichael, CA $10.0m.
VA Hospital, (Associated Architects),
Reno, NV $50.0m.
MRI Unit, Emergency Room, Cafeteria &
Nursing Unit Renovations,
Medical Center Sacramento,
University of California, Davis $6.5m.
Cardiac Cath Lab & Surgery Expansion,
N.T. Enloe Hospital, Chico, CA $2.0m.

Interior Design
Rancho Seco Technical Center,
Sacramento, CA $1.5m.
Chico Main Office Renovation,
Pacific Bell $0.90m.
Cardiovascular Surgery Center,
Sacramento, CA $0.35m.
IBM Interior Renovation,
Sacramento, CA $2.0m.

Governmental
Rancho Seco Technical Center,
Sacramento Municipal Utility District,
Sacramento, CA $12.0m.
USPS General Mail Facility,
Stockton, CA $16.0m.
USPS General Mail Facility,
Sacramento, CA $50.0m.
Sacramento County Main Jail, (Associated
Architects), Sacramento, CA $80.0m.
El Dorado County Main Jail,
Placerville, CA $13.5m.
State Energy Commission Building,
Sacramento, CA $15.0m.

FIRM HISTORY
Nacht & Lewis Architects offer a complete range of professional design services including Research, Programming, Master Planning, Site Planning, Architectural Design, Interior Design, Contract Administration and Facilities Management.

Founded in 1922 by Leonard F. Starks AIA, the organization has been continuously engaged in the design of major projects such as schools, hospitals, commercial offices, criminal justice and public service buildings. Many of these were keystones of later community development.

With 62 people, Nacht & Lewis Architects is adequately sized to execute large projects, while still flexible to be effective on smaller projects. The firm's current location is a building designed by and constructed for Nacht & Lewis Architects and its primary consulting engineers. Proximity of the firms and close working relationships allow Nacht & Lewis Architects to provide all the advantages of a 150-person architectural/ engineering firm. Advantages include: comprehensive concept development, tightly coordinated documents; and rapid response to project requirements.

DESIGN PHILOSOPHY
Architecture at its best is a rational, well-conceived prototype created in response to a particular set of conditions. It is artistic, environmentally sensitive, and most of all appropriate.

Nacht & Lewis Architects is dedicated to the production of architecture at its best. The firm's standards of excellence in design have resulted in recognition from the industry, and numerous awards from the architectural profession.

Successful practice of architecture requires the ability to synthesize the many factors influencing a project: the site, environment, budget, the program, time constraints, and the technology of construction. However, it requires most the ability to interact with people.

The success of any building project is a measure of how well we have been able to work with the client toward the accurate definition of needs and goals. The success of any architectural practice is measured by this process repeated effectively over a period of years.

Our purpose as professionals is to effectively serve our client's needs, and, at the same time, enrich the life experience by bringing people into closer harmony with their environment - through architecture.

NBBJ

NBBJ

ESTABLISHED
1943

FEES FOR 1987
$39 million

NATIONAL RANKINGS
3rd in Architecture
(according to Building Design &
Construction)
2nd in Architecture
(according to Engineering News
Record)
9th in Health Care Architecture
(according to Modern Healthcare)
10th in Commercial Renovation
(according to Commercial
Renovation)

OFFICES
111 South Jackson Street
Seattle, WA 98104
Telephone (206) 223 5555

55 Nationwide Boulevard
Columbus, OH 43215
Telephone (614) 224 7145

6 North Atlantic Wharf
Charleston, SC 29401
Telephone (803) 577 2163

559 Jones Franklin Road
Suite 150
Waters Edge Office Park
Raleigh, NC 27606
Telephone (919) 851 8382

130 West 30th
Suite 1301
New York City, NY 10001
Telephone (212) 564 3098

620 North Country Club Road
Tucson, AZ 85716
Telephone (602) 795 0100

1661 East Camelback Road
Suite 179
Phoenix, AZ 85016
Telephone (602) 263 0699

130 Sutter Street
San Francisco, CA 94104
Telephone (415) 981 1100

1229 Greenwood Cliff
Suite 100
Charlotte, NC 28204
Telephone (704) 343 9900

PARTNERS
William Bain, FAIA
Friedrich Bohm, AIA, AICP
Lawrence Helman, AICP
David Hoedemaker, FAIA
James Jonassen, FAIA
John Pangrazio, AIA
David Zimmerman

NUMBER OF EMPLOYEES
425

PROJECT TYPES
Commercial
Criminal Justice
Health Care
Hospitality
Public Assembly
Retail
Technical Facilities

SUPPORT SERVICES
Economics
Graphic Design
Interiors
Landscape Architecture
Land Use Planning
Urban Design

NBBJ operates from a service philosophy
that works for us and our clients.
We know a service firm depends entirely
on the quality of its people, so we go out
of our way to attract the top of the
architectural profession. Because we
hire the best, we can deliver the best to
our clients. And getting the best people
working on your team guarantees value.

We know we can't be all things to all people,
so NBBJ concentrates on specialized areas,
excelling in each: health care, commercial,
high technology, interiors, retail, and
renovation. This keeps us focused -
and the best at what we do.

We design buildings to fit each client's
specific needs, so NBBJ projects never fit a
single pattern. Two Union Square towers 20
floors over neighboring One Union Square,
yet our design for the new 56-story Seattle
building creates a familial relationship that
strengthens the complex as a whole; our
addition to Louis Kahn's Salk Institute in San
Diego is a seamless extension of an
acknowledged architectural masterpiece.
We always find appropriate design solutions.
The NBBJ philosophy works. Our current
projects total over $1 billion in construction.
And that equals a lot of satisfied clients.

1

3

2

4

6

7

8

5

9

10

11

1. San Jose State University
   Library, San Jose, CA
2. Nevada National Bank,
   Reno, NV
3. University of San Francisco
   Health & Recreation Center
4. California Farm Bureau
   Headquarters, Sacramento, CA
5. Pflueger Architects Offices,
   "The Bathaus"
6. Marina Villas,
   San Francisco, CA
7. Paramount Theater, Oakland
8. Orchard Building
9. City College of San Francisco

10. Stanford University Tennis
    Stadium
11. Stanford University
    Environment and Safety
    Facilities

PFLUEGER ARCHITECTS, INC.

M. Pflueger   J. Pflueger

PFLUEGER ARCHITECTS, INC.

ESTABLISHED
Pflueger Architects Inc. 1987
Pflueger Architects 1976
Milton T. Pflueger 1946
Timothy L. Pflueger 1908

ADDRESS
165 Tenth Street
San Francisco, CA 94103

TELEPHONE
(415) 431 5630

FACSIMILE
(415) 431 1640

NUMBER OF EMPLOYEES
23

PROJECT TYPES
Commercial
Community
Educational
Governmental
Medical
Recreational
Resort/Theme Parks/Hotels
Residential

OTHER DISCIPLINES
Master Planning
Space Planning/Interior Design
Energy: Management, Passive
& Active Systems
Hazardous Waste
Programming/Facility Studies

PERSON TO CONTACT
John M. Pflueger

CURRENT & RECENT PROJECTS

Commercial
California Farm Bureau
Headquarters, Sacramento
Nevada National Bank
Headquarters

Community
California Academy of Sciences
Performing Arts Center,
Sierra Arts Foundation

Educational
Batmale Hall, City College of San Francisco
San Jose State University Library

Governmental
Administrative Headquarters,
U.S. Air Force, NV
U.S. Naval Brig, Treasure Island,
San Francisco

Historical Restoration
Bathhouse, Pflueger Architects
Santa Rosa Ferryboat

Medical
Ingleside Mental Health Center
Shriners Hospital for Crippled Children
Walter Reed General Hospital

Recreational
Koret Health & Recreation Center,
University of San Francisco
San Francisco Giants Baseball Stadium
Superbowl Improvements
Tennis Center, Stanford University

Residential
Marina Villas, San Francisco
Rounhill Apartments, Fairfield, CA

Resort
Farallon Hotel, San Francisco
Puako Condominiums, HI
Warfield Gateway Center, San Francisco

Master Planning
California Academy of Sciences
California Farm Bureau
City College of San Francisco
Mare Island, U.S. Navy
Treasure Island, U.S. Navy
University of San Francisco

Space Planning - Interior Design
California Farm Bureau Headquarters
Nevada National Bank, Reno, NV
Santa Rosa Ferryboat, San Francisco

Energy
Bank of America/Pacific Gas & Electrical
- Energy Manual
Merritt-Peralta Co-Generation
Crockett Co-Generation
University of San Francisco Co-Generation

Hazardous Waste
Environmental Safety Facility, Stanford

HISTORY
Pflueger Architects was organized in 1907. The firm was responsible for Union Square Plaza and Garage, 450 Sutter Building, Pacific Coast Stock Exchange, Top of the Mark, I. Magnin, Pacific Telephone Building and participation in the design of the Bay Bridge and the 1939 World's Fair. In 1929, Milton Pflueger joined his brother Timothy. Upon Timothy Pflueger's death in 1946, the firm became Milton T. Pflueger, AIA, Architect. The firm's work under Milton's direction included civic centers for the cities of Richmond, Sunnyvale, and Modesto; projects for Stanford University, University of San Francisco, City College of San Francisco, and Holy Names College; and medical facilities for Shriners Hospital for Crippled Children, Alta Bates, and the University of California Medical Center. He was also the managing principal of the joint venture for Oakland Naval Hospital, Letterman General Hospital, Silas B. Hayes Hospital at Fort Ord, and the New Walter Reed General Hospital in Washington, DC

John Pflueger joined the firm in 1961. In 1976, Milton and John Pflueger became partners to form the firm of Pflueger Architects. Under the leadership of John Pflueger, the firm has become an acknowledged national leader in quality design solutions and energy efficient buildings which include: Nevada National Bank Headquarters in Reno; the California Farm Bureau Federation Office Building in Sacramento; San Jose State University Library. Continuing projects at Stanford University, University of San Francisco, Holy Names College, City College of San Francisco, and California Academy of Sciences have been completed along with major urban centers such as the Farallon Hotel and Warfield Gateway Center in San Francisco.

PHILOSOPHY OF THE FIRM
We place special emphasis on producing simple, strong, energy-conscious solutions. Effective project management insures conformance with schedule and budget. The variety of completed projects for clients on a continuing basis illustrates our fulfillment of client objectives with completely successful projects.

Responses are immediate, schedule and budget are met, and the maximum expertise and full resources of the firm are committed to each project.

Our philosophy is one which states that each project is as unique in its special requirements and goals as the personalities of the client team. We treat each project with a fresh approach. There are no preconceived solutions, rather the expertise of the design team gained from an eighty-year history of meeting client needs by developing the unique and special solutions each project requires.

National Semiconductor
Employee Park, Santa Clara, CA

Royston Hanamoto Alley & Abey Office, Mill Valley, CA

University of California Quarry
Theater, Santa Cruz, CA

Cuesta Park, MountainView, CA

Taman Kiara (National Arboretum) Kuala Lumpur, Malaysia

Central Park, Santa Clara, CA

ROYSTON HANAMOTO ALLEY & ABEY

ROYSTON HANAMOTO ALLEY & ABEY
Landscape Architects and Planners

ESTABLISHED DATE
1958

ADDRESS
225 Miller Avenue
Mill Valley, CA 94942-0937

TELEPHONE
(415) 383 7900

FACSIMILE
(415) 383 1433

DIRECTORS
Robert N. Royston, FASLA
Asa Hanamoto, FASLA
Louis G. Alley, AIA
Kazuo Abey, ASLA
Patricia A. Carlisle, ASLA
Harold N. Kobayashi, ASLA

NUMBER OF EMPLOYEES
30

PROJECT TYPES
Environmental Planning
Park and Recreation Design
Long Range Park Systems Planning
Park Rehabilitation and Restoration
Zoo and Museum
Community Planning and Housing
Resort and Hotel
Educational Facilities
Urban Planning and Design
Commercial and Professional
Industrial and Research Facilities
Large Industrial Facility Master
Planning
Transportation Systems
Historic Preservation and
Restoration
Land and Water Reclamation
Cemeteries and Religious Facilities

RELATED SERVICES
Multidisciplinary Team
Management
Design Guidelines
Landscape Maintenance
Guidelines
Public Participation Programs
Computer Applications

PERSON TO CONTACT
Asa Hanamoto
Louis G. Alley

CURRENT AND RECENT PROJECTS

Park and Recreation Design
Westminster Park, Westminster, CO
Central Park, Santa Clara, CA
Cuesta Park, Mountain View, CA
Boeddeker Park, San Francisco, CA
National Semiconductor Employee Park, CA
National Arboretum, Kuala Lumpur,
Malaysia

System Wide Park Master Plans
City of Denver Parks Master Plan, CO
San Luis Obispo County, CA
City of Santa Barbara, CA

Zoo and Museum
San Francisco Zoo Primate Center, CA
San Francisco Zoo Lion House, CA
Coyote Point Museum, San Mateo, CA
Jurong Bird Park, Singapore

Community Planning and Housing
Murrayhill New Community, Beaverton, OR
Summerlin New Community, Las Vegas, NV
North Bonneville New Town, WA
Vail Community Plan, Vail, CO
Harbor Bay Isle, Alameda, CA
Smith Ranch Homes, San Rafael, CA
Robert Mondavi Residence, Napa Valley, CA

Resort and Hotel
Sunriver Resort and Community,
Sunriver, OR
Marriott S. F. Airport Hotel, Burlingame, CA
Marriott Yerba Buena Hotel,
San Francisco, CA
Harbor Bay Isle Club, Alameda, CA
Sentosa Island, Singapore

Education
U of Oregon Science Facility, Eugene, OR
U of New Mexico Valencia Campus, NM
U C Berkeley Bechtel Engineering
Center, CA
U of Utah, Salt Lake City, UT
De Anza College, Cupertino, CA
San Joaquin Delta College, Stockton, CA
Reichold Center Amphitheater, College of
Virgin Islands
U C Santa Cruz Quarry Amphitheater, CA

Urban Planning and Design
Holocaust Memorial, San Francisco, CA
Alhambra Main Street Beautification, CA
San Rafael Fourth Street Beautification, CA
Mill Valley Plaza, Mill Valley, CA

Commercial and Professional
Bishop Ranch, San Ramon, CA
Sierra Point Koll Center, Brisbane, CA
Stanford Children's Hospital, Stanford, CA

Industrial and Research
Oceanside Pollution Control Plant,
San Francisco, CA
Sandia National Laboratories
Master Plan, NM
Skywalker Ranch/Lucasfilm,
San Rafael, CA

Transportation Systems
SFBART Stations, Line & Yards, CA
Alma/Cahill CALTRAIN Stations,
San Jose, CA
Vail Transportation Terminal, Vail, CO

Reclamation and Historic Restoration
Carmel Beach Restoration, Carmel, CA
Olompali State Park, Marin County, CA
California State Railroad Museum,
Sacramento

Cemeteries
V A National Cemetery, Riverside, CA
V A San Joaquin Valley National
Cemetery, CA
Parque Del Recuerdo, Santiago, Chile
Pusara Negara, Kuala Lumpur, Malaysia

PROFILE
Royston Hanamoto Alley & Abey is a
professional landscape architecture and
planning firm which offers its clients
resources and expertise which are unique to
the profession. The firm has been a leader
in the field for over three decades, providing
creative, innovative, and responsive design
solutions for a wide range of national and
international clients. The practice
encompasses all aspects of landscape
architecture and planning.

HISTORY
Founded as a partnership between Robert
Royston, Asa Hanamoto and David Mayes in
June 1958, the practice continues to grow
and provide professional services of the
highest quality. Over one hundred national
and local design awards attest to the success
of the firm's work.

PHILOSOPHY
In each project, Royston Hanamoto Alley &
Abey strives for design solutions which are a
synthesis of human values and aspirations,
natural and cultural form determinants
unique to each site, and functional and
economic influences. Their mission has
been to enhance and to preserve the
landscape and environment for people to
use and respect. Underlying the work of the
firm is the basic philosophy of searching for
timeless solutions while allowing the
projects to be completed on schedule within
approved budgets. A guiding belief of the
firm is that the highest quality of design
results from a continual involvement of the
principals with the client and a talented,
closely integrated technical staff throughout
the design process. Their desire is to
continually improve their capability in the
field of environmental design and remain a
constant source of human creativity in a
world dominated by technology.

RTKL

1

2

3

4

5

1. A mixed-use complex in West Palm Beach, Florida, Esperante pairs a 20-story high-rise structure with a tiered, four-story pavilion complex connected by an atrium courtyard.

2. Exposed steel space frames in the public areas and a tent-covered food court create an open-air feeling in Town Center at Boca Raton, an award-winning Florida mall.

3. The Grand Hyatt Washington, DC features a lofty atrium courtyard with indoor pond, abundant landscaping, and theatrical lighting.

4. Darling Harbourside's vaulted pavilions and public promenade offer a lively environment for visitors to Sydney's magnificent harbor.

5. With its intricate combination of facets and setbacks, the 24-story Signet Tower etches a distinctive signature on Baltimore's skyline.

RTKL ASSOCIATES INC.

ESTABLISHED DATE
1946

ADDRESSES
400 East Pratt Street
Baltimore, MD 21202
Telephone   (301) 528 8600
Facsimile   (301) 385 2455

2828 Routh Street
Suite 200, LB 34
Dallas, TX 75201
Telephone   (214) 871 8877
Facsimile   (214) 871 7023

1140 Connecticut Avenue, N.W.
Suite 300
Washington, DC 20036
Telephone   (202) 833 4400
Facsimile   (202) 887 5168

One East Broward Boulevard
Fort Lauderdale, FL 33301
Telephone   (305) 764 0500
Facsimile   (305) 764 1960

818 West Seventh Street
Los Angeles, CA 90017
Telephone   (213) 627 7373
Facsimile   (213) 627 9815

DIRECTORS
Harold L. Adams, FAIA - Chairman
George J. Pillorgé, FAIA, AICP
- Vice Chairman
Joseph J. Scalabrin, AIA
- Vice Chairman
Robert J. Kolker, PE
- Senior Vice President
Robert R. Manfredi, PE
- Senior Vice President
Ted Niederman, AIA
- Senior Vice President
S. Thomas Wheatley III, AIA
- Senior Vice President

NUMBER OF EMPLOYEES
563; includes 28 principals

PROJECT TYPES
Conference Centers
Government
Hotels
Interiors
Medical
Mixed-use
Office
Retail

OTHER DISCIPLINES
Architecture
Engineering (civil/electrical/
mechanical/structural)
Graphics
Interior design
Planning
Urban design

PERSON TO CONTACT
Firmwide
Harold L. Adams, FAIA
Laurin McCracken, AIA
Baltimore Office
George J. Pillorgé, FAIA
Dallas Office
Joseph J. Scalabrin, AIA
Washington, DC Office
Bernard J. Wulff, AIA
Ft. Lauderdale Office
Thomas C. Gruber, AIA
Los Angeles Office
S. Thomas Wheatley III, AIA

CURRENT AND RECENT PROJECTS
As a full-service, multi-disciplinary firm,
RTKL offers proven experience on all project
types, as evidenced by more than 80 local
and national awards of excellence. RTKL is
currently at work on more than 300 projects
world-wide, including an airline terminal
(Massachusetts); corporate education
center (Massachusetts); hotels (world-
wide); master plan for new sports complex
(Maryland); county government center
(Virginia); mixed-use plan for Los Angeles
Chinatown (California); major retail
developments in Australia, Brazil, and Japan;
resort developments in Japan; hotel in Brazil;
and master plan for 30-acre community near
Cairo, Egypt.

Recently completed projects include Darling
Harbourside (Sydney); the San Antonio
Marriott River Center (Texas); Esperante
mixed-use project (Florida); Westlake Mall
(Washington State); Bay Plaza waterfront
retail (Florida); Tysons Mall (Virginia);
interiors for Riggs Banks (Washington, DC)
and Bank of Baltimore Tower (Maryland);
planning and urban design for Mud Island
community (Tennessee); and historic
restoration work on Tudor Mansion
(Washington, DC). The following covers a
partial client list for various building types.

CLIENTS

Mixed-use and Retail
The Hooker Companies; Melvin Simon and
Associates; The Rouse Company, The
Lehndorff Group

Hotels
Marriott Corporation; The Hyatt
Corporation and Hyatt International; Ritz-
Carlton; Rosewood Hotels; Princess Hotels
International; and Radisson Hotels
Corporation

Corporate Facilities
The IBM Corporation; Digital Equipment
Corporation; Siemens; Cabot, Cabot &
Forbes; Maryland National Bank; Tishman-
Speyer Properties; Trammell Crow
Company; and Travelers Insurance
Company

Planning and Urban Design
City of Arlington, Texas; City of San Jose,
California; City of Clearwater, Florida; City of
Baltimore, Maryland; City of Cincinnati,
Ohio; District of Columbia Redevelopment
Land Agency; Reston (Virginia) Land
Development Corporation; The Pyramid
Companies; Pennsylvania Avenue
Development Corporation, Washington, DC

Interiors
The IBM Corporation; The World Bank;
Riggs Bank; Citibank; and Peat Marwick

Health Care
The Johns Hopkins Medical Institutions; the
University of Maryland Medical Systems;
Hartford Hospital; and The National
Institutes of Health

DESIGN PHILOSOPHY AND HISTORY
Founded in 1946 as a two-man office, RTKL
has grown steadily over the years and now
boasts over 500 employees in five offices
across the United States. The firm's studios
are under the direction of principals who
guide projects from inception through
construction. With the support of the most
advanced computer-aided design and
drafting (CADD) systems available,
architects assigned to a given studio work in
close cooperation with RTKL's mechanical/
electrical, structural, and civil engineers,
interior architects, and graphic designers.
This collaboration fosters cooperation,
efficiency, and the creation of the best
product possible.

RTKL takes pride in its record of delivering
projects on time and within budget, a record
achieved by constant review of schedules
and expenditures and by the use of fast-track
and phased construction techniques.
Working closely with clients to achieve
optimum levels of economy and design,
RTKL designs projects that are
characterized by low operating costs and
long life-cycles -- quality architecture that
makes a strong and lasting statement.

1

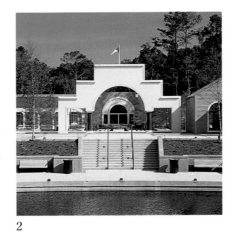

2

3

1. ALR Office
   Oakland, CA

2. Kiawah Town Center
   Kiawah Island, SC

3. Key Colony
   Key Biscayne, FL

4. Fisher Island
   Miami, FL

5. Flax Residence
   Healdsburg, CA

4

5

SANDY & BABCOCK INC

SANDY & BABCOCK INC
Architecture Planning
& Interior Design

ESTABLISHED
1960

OFFICES
1349 Larkin Street
P.O. Box 640777
San Francisco, CA 94164-0777
Telephone (415) 673 8990
Facsimile (415) 441 3767

2300 South Dixie Highway
Miami, FL 33133
Telephone (305) 856 2021
Facsimile (305) 856 0854

DIRECTORS
Donald Sandy, FAIA
Chairman
James A. Babcock
President
John F. Eller, AIA
Chief Executive Officer
Frederic L. Schaefer
Chief Financial Officer and General Counsel

NUMBER OF EMPLOYEES
50

INQUIRIES TO
John Eller in San Francisco
Ron Pales in Miami

PROFILE

Sandy & Babcock Inc routinely manages large-scale resort, mixed-use and residential projects throughout the United States and overseas. Because our work covers a broad geographic area, we take great care to design locally-sensitive buildings which draw their texture, scale and color from the surrounding building styles and site conditions. Combined with this emphasis on quality design is our ability to work within the parameters of the project as defined by the client's program and budgetary considerations. The success of this commitment is evidenced by such developments as:

- Key Colony in Key Biscayne, Florida; an archetype of Sandy & Babcock's design philosophy, which is based on the premise that the solution is entirely within the problem . Key Colony was the first architecturally significant condominium project in the greater Miami area, awakening the developer community to the financial rewards for the extra efforts required to produce high-quality architecture.

- Fisher Island, a $900 million residential resort development in Miami, Florida. This self-sufficient community, created to provide a retreat for second-home buyers worldwide, has proven exceptionally successful in this highly-competitive luxury residential market.

- Kiawah Island Resort in South Carolina, for which the master planning and design of the residential and commercial components won much acclaim for their harmonious blend of architecture, function and site.

- Post Street Towers, which presented severe constraints with its sloping infill site. The parcel bisected an entire city block in downtown San Francisco bound by buildings on both sides. The solution accommodated the client's requirement for 250 apartment units, while retaining an appropriate scale to the neighboring buildings and a respect for the fabric of the neighborhood. Again, this project has been an enormous financial success for the project's developers.

Sandy & Babcock Inc continues to strive for design excellence and to maintain its position at the forefront of the profession, as recognized by the 130 national awards the firm has received for excellence in design.

Current projects on our boards and under construction include:

Little Bay Resort: Master planning and design for a 263-acre resort on Montserrat, British West Indies.

Island Park: Master planning and design for a 67-acre mixed-use complex in Belmont, California.

Golf Course Resorts: Master planning for numerous PGA-golf-course resorts around the country, including: Tampa, Florida; San Antonio, Texas; Hawaii; Potomac, Maryland; Seattle, Washington; and Ventura, San Diego, and the San Francisco Bay Area in California.

Grossinger's Resort: The refurbishment of an established resort in Liberty, New York, which involves master planning 900 acres, rehabilitation of the original hotel, and the design of five phases of new residential development.

Friar's Bay: Master planning and conceptual design for a 270-acre world class resort on St. Kitts, British West Indies.

King's Bay: Master planning and initial design for 300 water-oriented luxury condominiums, with a club house, tennis courts and 18-hole golf course in Miami, Florida.

Cheeca Lodge: Refurbishment of an oceanfront hotel in Islamorada, Florida, and design of an additional 128 guest units in low-rise villas.

Fisher Island: From design through construction administration, work continues on the various commercial and residential phases of this 216-acre island resort off the southern tip of Miami Beach.

We value the many long-standing relationships we have formed with our clients. With our staff of dedicated senior architects, we provide the broad base of knowledge, experience, and creativity they need to achieve their goals.

PHOTO CREDITS:
1. Russell Abraham; 2. David Soliday;
3&4. Steven Brooke; 5. Chris Larrance

1. 388 Market Street, San Francisco, CA, USA
2. Texas Commerce Tower, Dallas, TX, USA
3. Sears Tower, Chicago, IL, USA
4. Rowes Wharf, Boston, MA, USA
5. United Gulf Bank, Manama, Bahrain
6. 1992 World's Fair (Project), Chicago, IL, USA
7. Palio Restaurant, New York City, NY, USA
8. Haj Terminal, King Abdul Aziz International Airport, Jeddah, Saudi Arabia
9. Kuwait Chancery, Washington, DC, USA
10. Broadgate, London, England
11. The Grand Hotel, Washington, DC, USA
12. Arlington Park International Racecourse, Arlington Heights, IL, USA

1

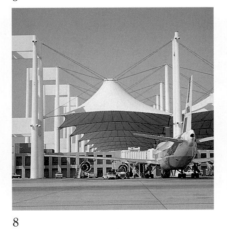

2

3

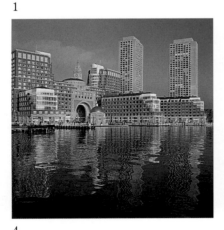

4

5

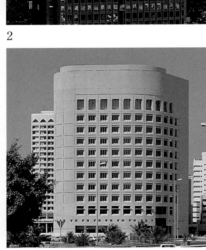

6

7

8

9

10

11

12

SKIDMORE, OWINGS & MERRILL

SKIDMORE, OWINGS & MERRILL

ESTABLISHED

1936

ADDRESSES

Chicago
33 West Monroe Street
Chicago, IL 60603-5373 USA
Telephone (312) 641 5959
Facsimile (312) 332 5632

Los Angeles
725 South Figueroa Street
10th Floor
Los Angeles, CA 90017 USA
Telephone (213) 488 9700
Facsimile (213) 488 0488

New York
220 East 42nd Street
New York, NY 10017-5806 USA
Telephone (212) 309 9500
Facsimile (212) 309 9750

San Francisco
333 Bush Street
San Francisco, CA 94104-2814 USA
Telephone (415) 981 1555
Facsimile (415) 398 3214

Washington, DC
1201 Pennsylvania Avenue, N.W.
Washington, DC 20004-2401 USA
Telephone (202) 393 1400
Facsimile (202) 662 2323

London, England
Skidmore, Owings & Merrill, Inc.
Devonshire House,
9th Floor, Mayfair Place
London WIX-5FH ENGLAND
Telephone 011 44 1 930 9711
Facsimile 011 44 1 629 1287

PARTNERS

Karen B. Alschuler, MCP, AICP
Robert B. Armsby, BArch, MArch, AIA
David M. Childs, MArch, FAIA
Raymond J. Clark,
BScME, MScME, PE, CIBSE
Walter H. Costa, BArch, MArch, FAIA
Raul de Armas, BArch, AIA
Lawrence S. Doane, BArch, FAIA
William M. Drake, MArch, AIA, RIBA
Thomas J. Eyerman,
BArch, MBA, FAIA, RIBA
Thomas K. Fridstein, BArch, MBA, AIA
Richard A. Giegengack, MArch, AIA
Joseph A. Gonzalez, BArch, AIA
Bruce J. Graham, BArch, FAIA, RIBA
Parambir S. Gujral,
BSc, MScME, PE, IES, CIBSE
Robert A. Halvorson,
BScCE, MScSE, PE, ASCE
Craig W. Hartman, BArch, AIA
Alan D. Hinklin, BArch, AIA
Robert P. Holmes, MArch, AIA
Robert A. Hutchins, MArch, AIA
Srinivasa Iyengar,
BE, MHSE, MCSE, FASCE, FIStructE
Richard C. Keating, BArch, FAIA
D. Stanton Korista,
BScCE, MScCE, FASCE

John L. Kriken,
BArch, MArch, FAIA, AICP
Diane Legge, MArch, AIA
Michael A. McCarthy,
BArch, MArch, FAIA
Leon Moed, BArch, AIA
Adrian D. Smith, BArch, FAIA, RIBA
Donald C. Smith,
BArch, MArch, FAIA, RIBA
Kenneth A. Soldan,
BArch, MSc(Arch), AIA
Douglas F. Stoker,
BArch, MBA, AIA, IFMA
Marilyn Jordan Taylor, MArch, AIA
Richard F. Tomlinson,
BArchEng, MArch, AIA
Robert Turner, BArch, AIA, RIBA
Robert L. Wesley,
BScArchEng, MArch, AIA
John H. Winkler,
BArch, MUrbanDes, AIA
Carolina Y.C. Woo,
BArch, MBusPol, FAIA, RIBA

CONSULTING PARTNER

Marc E. Goldstein, BArch, MArch, FAIA

NUMBER OF EMPLOYEES

1,600

PROJECT TYPES

Office Buildings
Banks
Commercial Buildings
Schools
Universities
Libraries
Government Buildings
Hotels
Hospitals
Industrial Buildings
Airports
Railway Stations
Subways
Exposition Centers
Sporting Arenas
Racecourses
Concert Halls
Theatres
Restaurants and Clubs
Stores and Shops
Houses of Worship
Residential Buildings
Urban Multi-Use Complexes

DISCIPLINES

Architecture
Urban and Environmental Planning
Environmental Analysis
Site Planning
Landscape Architecture
Civil Engineering
Structural Engineering
Mechanical/Electrical Engineering
Plumbing/Fire Safety Engineering
Interior Architecture
Space Planning
Facilities Programming
Equipment Planning
Field Observation
Computer Capabilities
Graphics
Estimating
Specifications

FIRM PROFILE

The partnership of Louis Skidmore and Nathaniel Owings was formed in 1936, after both had worked together on the design of the 1933 Chicago World's Fair, "A Century of Progress". Skidmore set up the New York office in 1937, and went to work on the planning and design of the 1939 New York World's Fair. Skidmore and Owings soon decided to broaden the scope of their practice to include engineering services, and John Merrill, an architectural engineer joined the partnership in 1939.

SOM made its first really major impact on the architectural and planning profession in the 1940's, when the firm received the commission to plan and design Oak Ridge, Tennessee, an entire new town serving the Manhattan Project, which developed the first atomic bomb. In 1946, SOM was asked to design Mount Zion Hospital in San Francisco, which led to the opening of an office there. With a national presence and a reputation for executing large commissions well established, SOM entered the 1950's as a major force in American architecture. The landmark Lever House in New York, completed in 1952, earned the firm world-wide recognition for the high quality of its designs. SOM became famous for its corporate towers which altered the skylines of countless cities, culminating with the world's tallest building, the Sears Tower in Chicago, which was completed in 1974.

In 1963, the renowned architectural historian Henry-Russell Hitchcock wrote that the *"major significance of SOM's architecture...[is] to be measured by its relationship to the central building problem of our day...the rebuilding of our cities and, in the underdeveloped areas of the world, the creation of new ones."* In the 1970's and 1980's, the firm firmly established its ability to be measured by Hitchcock's standard, with mixed-use urban complexes such as Rowes Wharf in Boston and large-scale planning and urban design projects such as Canary Wharf in London, England.

In 1950, SOM was the first firm to be chosen for exhibition at the Museum of Modern Art in New York. The accompanying catalogue noted that the firm "produces imaginative, serviceable, and sophisticated architecture deserving of special attention." SOM has maintained this reputation, and, in recognition of the firm's achievements as a group of professionals working together, the American Institute of Architects awarded its first Architectural Firm Award for excellence in design in 1962.

An unyielding commitment to excellence has consistently produced visionary architectural, design, planning and technical performance, and the firm has been rewarded with over 500 awards for quality and innovation.

SPRANKLE, LYND & SPRAGUE, ARCHITECTS
Architecture
Planning
Landscape
Interiors

ESTABLISHED
1958

ADDRESS
33 New Montgomery
Suite 890
San Francisco, CA 94105

TELEPHONE
(415) 543 1616

FACSIMILE
(415) 974 6625

PRINCIPALS
Dale F. Sprankle, AIA
John S. Lynd, AIA
Robert B. Sprague, AIA

ASSOCIATE PRINCIPALS
Gary R. Frye, AIA
Gregory Di Paolo, AIA

ASSOCIATES
David Dobereiner, AIA
Brian L. Johnson, AIA

PROJECTS
Conrad International Hotel,
Convention Center and Jupiters Casino,
Gold Coast, Queensland, Australia

Mori Meadowland Center,
Meadowlands, NJ

Parkland College, Champaign, IL

Corporate Headquarters, California Casualty
Management Co., San Mateo, CA

Lake Tahoe Community College,
South Lake Tahoe, CA

The Cedars Executive Conference Center,
New Brunswick, NJ

California School for the Deaf, Fremont, CA

Southgate Office Towers, Sheraton Hotel,
Festival Retail and Condominiums,
Melbourne, Victoria, Australia

Master Plan and Administration Building,
St. Mary's College, Moraga, CA

Chadstone Shopping Mall, Melbourne,
Victoria, Australia

Student Services Building, California State
University, San Luis Obispo, CA

Herbert Hoover Federal Memorial Building,
Stanford University

Myer Centre Mall, Brisbane,
Queensland, Australia

WFTV - Channel 9 Television Station,
Orlando, FL

Flint Center for the Performing Arts,
Cupertino, CA

Las Colinas Master Plan, Dallas, TX

Media Arts Center-Pacific Gas & Electric,
San Francisco, CA

Center for the Study of Language &
Information, Stanford University

Air-Ocean Sciences Center, Naval
Postgraduate School, Monterey, CA

KTVU - Channel 2 Television Station,
Oakland, CA

University of Santa Clara - Master Plan,
Santa Clara, CA

Greenfield College, Greenfield, MA

William M. Staerkel Theater and
Planetarium, Champaign, IL

College of the Virgin Islands, St. Thomas
and St. Croix Campuses, U.S. Virgin Islands

PROFILE
Sprankle, Lynd & Sprague has developed an
architectural practice dedicated to creative
design and strongly led professional
services for projects throughout the United
States and overseas. With our principal
office in San Francisco, we carry out much of
our out-of-state and international work
through highly successful collaboration and
association with local design professionals.

Our client's requirements and the
environment of their project are approached
as a whole. We seek to blend elements of
regionalism and indigenous architectural
character with programmatic functions to
create a meaningful and cohesive design
without ostentation.

Our diversified practice has developed a
breadth of experience in a broad range of
projects for both the public and private
sectors. These projects include hotels and
resorts, office and retail complexes, colleges
and universities, television studios, theaters,
scientific and computer facilities and master
planning for new communities.

To strengthen our methodology, we exploit
the flexibility of computer graphics for
conceptual development and presentation
and utilize the precision of CAD for
production processes.

1

2

3

4

5

1. 222 Berkeley Street, Boston
   Rendering by Frank M. Constantino.
   Copyright Robert A.M. Stern Architects.

2. St. Paul's School Library, NH
   Rendering by Andrew Zega.
   Copyright Robert A.M. Stern Architects.

3. Grand Harbor: Courtyard Houses, FL
   Copyright Robert A.M. Stern Architects.

4. Mexx International Headquarters, The Netherlands
   Peter Aaron. Copyright ESTO. Mamaroneck, New York.

5. Mexx International Headquarters, The Netherlands
   Peter Aaron. Copyright ESTO. Mamaroneck, New York.

Robert A.M. Stern (opposite page)
Photo credit: Barbra Walz

ROBERT A.M. STERN ARCHITECTS

Robert A.M. Stern

ROBERT A.M. STERN ARCHITECTS

ESTABLISHED
1969

ADDRESS
211 West 61st Street
New York, NY 10023

TELEPHONE
(212) 246 1980

FACSIMILE
(212) 246 2486

PRINCIPAL PARTNER
Robert A.M. Stern,
B.A., M. Arch., F.A.I.A.

MANAGING PARTNER
Robert S. Buford, Jr.,
B.A., M. Arch., A.I.A.

ASSOCIATES
Randy Correll, B.A., M. Arch.
Ellen Coxe,
B.A., M.S. Hist. Pres., M. Arch.
Robert Ermerins,
B.A., B.A. Arch., M. Arch.
Stephen T.B. Falatko,
B. Arch., M. Arch., A.I.A.
William T. Georgis, B.A., M. Arch.
Caryl Kinsey, B.S. Arch.
Thomas Kligerman, B.A., M. Arch.
Alex Lamis, S.B. Art & Design, M. Arch.
Armand LeGardeur, B.A., M. Arch.
Timothy E. Lenahan, B.A., M. Arch.
Grant Marani,
B. Arch., M. Arch., A.R.A.I.A.
Thomas Mellins, B.A., M.A.
Edward Ralston Mudd, B. Arch.,
M.S. Arch. & Urban Design, A.I.A.
Raul Morillas, B.F.A. Arch., B.L.A.
Barry Rice, Dip. Arch., B. Des. St.,
R.I.B.A., A.R.A.I.A.
Roger Seifter, B.A., M. Arch.
Elizabeth Thompson, B.A., B. Arch.,
M. Arch., Land. Arch. Cert., A.I.A.
Paul Whalen, B.A., M. Arch.
Graham Wyatt,
A.B. Summa, M. Arch., Dpl. Econ., A.I.A.

NUMBER OF EMPLOYEES
110

DISCIPLINES
Architecture
Urban Design and Master Planning
Interior Design
Landscape Design
Furniture and Decorative Arts

CURRENT AND RECENT PROJECTS

Commercial
Walt Disney Casting and Employment Center, Lake Buena Vista, FL; Disney Development Company. Construction Cost $8m.

Mexx International Headquarters, Voorschoten, The Netherlands; Mexx International, B.V. Construction Cost $10m.

222 Berkeley Street, Boston, MA; Gerald D. Hines Interests/The New England. Construction Cost $75m.

Point West Place Framingham, MA; Gerald D. Hines Interests. Construction Cost $7m.

Bancho House Tokyo, Japan; Kajima Corporation. Construction Cost, $10m.

90 Tremont Street, Boston, MA; St. James Properties. Construction Cost $50m.

Irvine Spectrum Office Properties, Irvine, CA; Bedford Properties. Construction Cost $6m.

Community
42nd Street Entertainment Centre, New York, NY; New York State Urban Development Corporation. Construction Cost $89.4m.

The Norman Rockwell Museum, Stockbridge, MA. Construction Cost $10m.

Synagogue for Congregation Kol Israel, Brooklyn, NY. Construction Cost $5.2m.

Educational
Mixed Use Tower, Manhattan School of Music, New York, NY; Continental/General Atlantic, MSM. Construction Cost $38m.

Library, St. Paul's School, Concord, NH. Construction Cost $8.6m.

Observatory Hill Dining Hall, Charlottesville, VA; University of Virginia. Construction Cost $1.25m.

Arts, Dance and Drama Facilities, University of California at Irvine. Construction Cost $1.5m.

Center for Jewish Life, Princeton University, NJ. Construction Cost $2.5m.

Residential Colleges Nine and Ten, University of California at Santa Cruz. Construction Cost N/A.

Brooklyn Law School, Brooklyn, NY. Construction Cost $18m.

Government
Police Headquarters, City of Pasadena, CA. Construction Cost $13m.

United States Embassy Office Annex, Budapest, Hungary; U.S. Department of State. Construction Cost N/A.

Medical Facilities
Bartholomew County Hospital, Columbus, IN. Construction Cost $48m.

Urban Design and Master Planning
Fine Arts Village, University of California at Irvine. Construction Cost N/A.

Squaw Valley USA, CA. Construction Cost N/A.

Santa Agueda Resort, Gran Canaria, Spain. Construction Cost N/A.

Recreational and Resort Developments
Beach Club Hotel and Yacht Club Hotel, FL. Construction Cost N/A.

Golf Club House, Izu Peninsula, Japan; Kajima Corporation. Construction Cost $9m.

Grand Harbor, Vero Beach, FL; Schaub Communities. Construction Cost $26m.

2 Star and 3 Star Resort Hotels, France. Construction Cost N/A.

Residential
Apartment Houses

Cap d'Akiya, Hayama, Japan; Sakuma International S.A. Construction Cost $4.2m.

Tegeler Hafen, Berlin, West Germany; Otembra GMBH. Construction Cost $1.5m.

Parcel G, Boston Fan Pier Development, Boston, MA; Hyatt Boston Carpenter Associates. Construction Cost $30m.

Residential Developments

The Hamptons, Lexington, MA; Boyd/Smith Inc. Construction Cost $3m.

Grace Estates, East Hampton, NY; The Greenberg Brother Partnership. Construction Cost $30m.

Custom Residences

Log Cabin, Old Snowmass, Aspen, CO
Residence, Red Mountain, Aspen, CO
Halpern Residence, Chestnut Hill, MA
Berggruen Residence, Russian Hill, San Francisco, CA
Hines Residence, River Oaks, Houston, TX
Planitzer Residence Fishers Island, NY

Interiors
Mexx Showroom, New York, NY; Mexx USA, Inc. Construction Cost $1.5m.

Capital Research Offices, New York, NY. Construction Cost $4.5m.

DESCRIPTION OF THE FIRM
Robert A.M. Stern Architects is a 110 person firm of architects, interior designers, landscape architects and support staff. Over its nineteen year history, the firm has established an international reputation as a leading design firm with wide experience in residential, commercial and institutional work. As the firm's practice has diversified, its geographical scope has widened to include projects in Europe, Asia and throughout the United States.

PERSON TO CONTACT
Robert S. Buford, Jr. - Managing Partner

Al-Sulaimania Shopping Center, Jeddah, Saudi Arabia

Mayapada Meridien Hotel, Jakarta, Indonesia

New York Hilton Hotel at Rockefeller Center

Royal Guest House (Designed as Hotel Inter-Continental), Jeddah, Saudi Arabia

Tahiti Rivnac Resort, Punaauia, Tahiti

Stouffer Hotel, Chicago, IL

WILLIAM B. TABLER ARCHITECTS

Principals

Associates

WILLIAM B. TABLER ARCHITECTS

ESTABLISHED DATE
1946

ADDRESS
333 Seventh Avenue
New York, NY 10001-5004

TELEPHONE
(212) 563 6960

FACSIMILE
(212) 563 3322

TELEX
224903

PRINCIPALS
William B. Tabler, FAIA
David P. Dann, AIA
Yoshiro Hashimoto, AIA
William B. Tabler, Jr., AIA

ASSOCIATES
Benjamin L. Hope
Michael A. Gawron
Gilbert Hickox
Eric M. Ohr

PROJECT TYPES
City center hotels
Luxury resorts
Conference centers
Office buildings
Mixed use complexes
Shopping centers
Hotel rehabilitation
University dormitories
Public schools
Private clubs

OTHER DISCIPLINES
Research and planning
Site selection and evaluation
Feasibility studies
Facilities programming
Construction management
Computer aided design
Consulting

CURRENT AND COMPLETED PROJECTS
Brooklyn Renaissance Plaza, NY
The Conrad Hotel, Istanbul, Turkey
Bally's Park Place Casino Hotel Guestroom Tower, Atlantic City, NJ
Izmir Hilton (International) Center, Izmir, Turkey
Waldorf Astoria Hotel Guestroom Remodeling, New York, NY
Royce-Carlin Conference Center, Huntington, NY
Ocean Place Hilton, Long Branch, NJ
Hotel Inter-Continental, New York, NY - Barclay Hotel Remodeling
Isla de Margarita Resort, Venezuela
Holiday Inn, Fort Lee, NJ
The Registry Resort, Scottsdale, AZ
Peninsula Hotel, Seoul, Korea
Rye Town Hilton, Rye, NY
Serena Hotel, Nairobi, Kenya
Hotel New Otani, Los Angeles, CA
Rio Othon Palace Hotel, Rio de Janeiro, Brazil
Harbour Castle Hotel, Toronto, Canada
Dorchester Hotel, Master Plan, London, England
Akasaka Prince Hotel, Tokyo, Japan
Caesar Park Hotel, Ipanema Beach, Rio de Janeiro, Brazil
Harvard Club Remodeling, New York, NY
Four Seasons Sheraton, Toronto, Canada
Hotel Condesa Del Mar, Acapulco, Mexico
Residence of the Korean Ambassador to the United Nations, New York, NY
Cala Di Volpe Hotel, Sardinia
Chosun Hotel, Seoul, Korea
Hapuna Beach Hotel, Hapuna, HI
The Washington Hilton Hotel, Washington, DC
Woodstock Inn and Resort, VT
Hotel Inter-Continental, Jerusalem
San Francisco Hilton Hotel, San Francisco, CA
Hotel Inter-Continental, Karachi, Pakistan
Narcotics Addiction Rehabilitation Centers, NY
Hotel Bonaventure, Montreal, Canada
Hotel Inter-Continental, Lusaka, Zambia

DESIGN PHILOSOPHY
Established over 40 years ago, the firm has designed 300 hotels on all continents except Antarctica. While the early emphasis was in the hospitality field, the current practice covers a wide range of project types.

William B. Tabler Architects is a design oriented firm. There is no recognizable "Tabler" style. Each design evolves individually reflecting the character of its environment.

DESIGN COMPETITIONS AWARDED
Meridien Hotel, Heliopolis, Cairo, Egypt - from seventy firms interviewed, six were invited to submit design solutions. Tabler was awarded first prize.

Host of Houston, Houston, TX - a design competition for hotel and theme building at the Intercontinental Airport. Tabler won.

Tahiti Rivnac Resort - six international architects submitted design solutions. Tabler was selected.

DESIGN COMMENDATIONS
The New York Hilton Hotel - design commended by Ada Louise Huxtable, New York Times.

The Washington Hilton - received critical acclaim from Wolf von Eckardt of the Washington Post for the successful design solution for a most difficult sloped site and the height limitation imposed by Washington, DC.

The Sheraton-Universal Hotel of the Stars, Los Angeles - architectural and structural design awards. The first seismic resistant ductile frame reinforced-concrete structure in the world. The frame was expressed in the facade by exposing sculpturally shaped structural elements reflecting the imposed stresses.

Inter-Continental Hotel, Jeddah, Saudi Arabia - His Majesty King Fahd felt it was worthy of a King's palace and commandeered it for his royal guest house.

The Tabler firm has been featured in over fifty publications - Time, Life, Architectural Record, Architectural Forum, Progressive Architecture, Interiors and more, plus many architectural books.

1
2
3
4
5
6
7
8

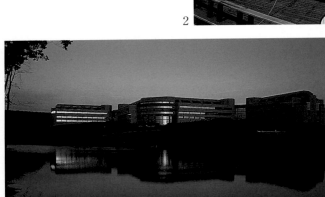

5

6
7

8

1. Countway Library of Medicine, Harvard University
2. Federal Reserve Bank of Boston
3. Westinghouse Furniture Systems Showroom
4. Singapore Treasury Building
5. Bristol-Myers Pharmaceutical Research Center
6. Citicorp Center
7. Huntington Avenue Footbridge, Copley Place
8. Carnegie Center

THE STUBBINS ASSOCIATES, INC.

**THE STUBBINS
ASSOCIATES, INC.**
Architecture, Planning,
Interior Design

ESTABLISHED
1949

ADDRESS
1033 Massachusetts Avenue
Cambridge, MA 02138

TELEPHONE
(617) 491 6450

FACSIMILE
(617) 491 7104

TELEX
(710) 320 1720 Stubbins Cam

DIRECTORS
Hugh Stubbins, FAIA
Richard Green, AIA
W. Easley Hamner, AIA
Merle T. Westlake, AIA
Michael J. Kraus, AIA
Howard E. Goldstein, AIA
Philip J. Goldberg
C. Ronald Ostberg, AIA
Peter J. Scott, AIA
Philip T. Seibert, IBD, ASID

NUMBER OF EMPLOYEES
100

DISCIPLINES
Architecture
Master Planning
Urban Design
Landscape Design
Interior Design
Graphic Design

PERSON TO CONTACT
Richard Green, AIA-President

DESIGN PHILOSOPHY

Established in 1949, The Stubbins
Associates brings to the complex demands
of professional practice extensive
experience in a broad range of building
types and planning solutions. Professional
services include feasibility studies,
programming, master planning,
architectural, interior and landscape design,
construction documents including
computer-aided design drafting (CADD),
and construction administration.

Directed by six principals, the firm
comprises highly qualified and experienced
professionals who take great pride in the
successful completion of each project. The
size and structure of the firm guarantee that
one of the principals directs each project. In
addition, a project director and project
designer are assigned to assure continuity
with the client and liaison with the
interdisciplinary team of professional
consultants.

Recognizing a responsibility to both our
clients and to the creative exploration of new
ideas, The Stubbins Associates does not
impose preconceived design solutions or
stylistic inclinations. Each building program
and specific context raises its own unique
problems and requires a unique solution.
Deep respect for our clients' knowledge of
their needs is tempered by the belief that
expressed functional requirements should
be viewed in the context of an often
unexpressed desire for something more --
the immeasurable quality that lifts the
human spirit.

The Stubbins Associates' reputation for
design excellence was formally
acknowledged when the firm received the
American Institute of Architects' highest
honor - the Architectural Firm Award - in
1967.

CLIENT LISTING

Mitsubishi Estate Co., Ltd
Bristol-Myers Company
The Polaroid Corporation
Hewlett Packard
The Cousteau Society
The MITRE Corporation
Cabot Corporation
Boston Design Center
Westinghouse Furniture Systems
General Cinema Corporation
Maersk Inc.
AT&T
NYNEX Business Information Systems
Development Bank of Singapore
Citibank
Federal Reserve Bank of Boston
Bank One
BayBank/Harvard Trust
Bank of Boston
The Prudential Insurance Company
Erie Insurance Group
Atlantic Mutual Companies
Marriott Corporation
Bally's Park Place Casino Hotel
Harrah's Marina Hotel Casino
General Services Administration
Metropolitan Dade County
Trammel Crow Company
JMB/Urban Investment &
Development Co.
The Hillman Company
Morstan Development Company
Meredith & Grew
Cabot, Cabot & Forbes
John W. Galbreath and Company
The Beacon Companies
Fisher Brothers
Carnegie Center Associates
Harvard University
Princeton University
The University of Chicago
Duke University
Vanderbilt University
Cornell University
Hamilton College
Massachusetts Institute of Technology
Tufts University
University of Massachusetts
Brandeis University
University of California at Santa Cruz
University of Virginia
Mount Holyoke College
Columbia University Teachers College
Bowdoin College

2

3

4

1

1. The Four Seasons Hotel, Newport Beach,
   Newport Beach, California
2. Hotel Bora Bora, French Polynesia
3. The Ritz-Carlton, Laguna Niguel, Laguna Niguel, California
4. The Sheraton Hobart Hotel, Tasmania, Australia

WIMBERLY ALLISON TONG & GOO

**WIMBERLY ALLISON
TONG & GOO**
Architects and Planners

ESTABLISHED
1945

OFFICES
2222 Kalakaua Avenue, Penthouse
Honolulu, HI 96815
Telephone (808) 922 1253
Facsimile (808) 922 1250
Telex 8704 WATG HR
Contact: George Berean

140 Newport Center Drive,
Suite 200
Newport Beach, CA 92660
Telephone (714) 759 8923
Facsimile (714) 759 3473
Telex 294695 WATG HR
Contact: Ron Holecek

Helber Hastert & Kimura
Planners
Grosvenor Center
733 Bishop Street, Suite 2590
Honolulu, HI 96813
Telephone (808) 545 2055
Facsimile (808) 545 2050
Telex 634468 HHVHK UW
Contact: Larry Helber

FOUNDER
George Wimberly, FAIA

PRINCIPALS
Gerald Allison, FAIA
Gregory Tong, AIA
Donald Goo, FAIA
Donald Fairweather
George Berean, AIA
Ronald Holecek, AIA
Sidney Char, AIA
Michael Chun, AIA
Donald Lee, AIA
Patrick Lawrence, AIA
Larry Helber, ASLA
Mark Hastert, AICP
Glenn Kimura

NUMBER OF EMPLOYEES
150

PROJECT TYPES
Hotels and Resorts
Mixed Use Developments
Office and Retail
Condominiums and Housing
Tourism/Resort Planning
Community Planning
Waterfront Planning
Transportation Planning

The Ritz-Carltons at Laguna Niguel and Rancho Mirage, California and Naples, Florida; The Hilton Hawaiian Village master plan and renovation, Honolulu; The Grand Floridian Beach Resort at Walt Disney World, Florida; Shangri-La Garden Wing, Singapore; The Regent of Bangkok, Thailand; Hotel Bora Bora, French Polynesia: these world renowned hotels and resorts are among facilities designed for the leisure and travel industry by Wimberly Allison Tong & Goo.

In over 40 years of practice, the firm has been the architects for an extraordinary range of projects representing more than 20,000 guest rooms in 25 countries around the world. WAT&G's hallmark is its commitment to design in context with its environment and in a manner supportive of both operator and developer objectives.

"Architecture is the setting for dreams" - a consistent theme in hotel operators' advertising which attracts visitors to WAT&G-designed resort and hotel projects throughout the world.

"It was remarkable to have taken on such a large project and have it compare to anything, anywhere in the world. (The renovation of The Hilton Hawaiian Village) was a very complex problem with an outstanding solution."

- Hawaii Renaissance Jury

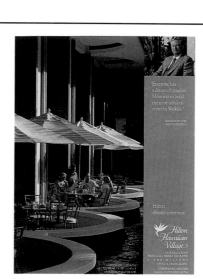

"The Grand Floridian is an inspired adaptation of elements from great American turn-of-the-century hotels..."
- Architectural Review

"Singapore's Shangri-La Hotel Garden Wing is a milestone in the history of the hotel industry."
- The Straits Times

2

1

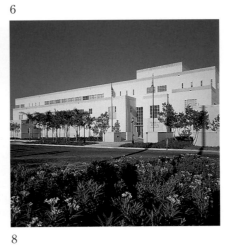

3

6

4

5

7

8

1. Grove Harbour (Architecture-Engineering)

2. The Mall at 163rd Street
(Architecture-Engineering-Interiors)

3. Racal-Milgo Corporate Headquarters
and Electronics Manufacturing
Complex (Architecture-Engineering)

4. Orbiter Mate-Demate Device for NASA's
Space Shuttle Program (Engineering)

5. Sonesta Sanibel Harbour Resort
(Construction Management)

6. Pompano Business Park
(Architecture-Engineering-Interiors)

7. South Florida Evaluation & Treatment
Center (Architecture-Engineering-Interiors)

8. City of Hialeah Police Administration
Building (Architecture-Engineering-Interiors)

WOLFBERG/ALVAREZ & ASSOCIATES
Architecture/Engineering/
Interior Design

ADDRESSES
Headquarters Office
5960 S.W. 57th Avenue
Miami, FL 33143
Telephone (305) 666 5474
Facsimile   (305) 666 5474

Northeast Regional Office
Suite 230
2000 North 14th Street
Arlington, VA 22201
Telephone (703) 276 7803
Facsimile   (703) 276 7803

PRINCIPALS
David A. Wolfberg, AIA
Julio E. Alvarez, P.E.

MANAGING ASSOCIATES
Marcel R. Morlote, AIA
Jose Mola, P.E.
Michael Konopka, AIA
Northeast Regional Office

NUMBER OF EMPLOYEES
125

DISCIPLINES
Architecture
Engineering
    Civil, Structural, Electrical
    & Mechanical
Interior Design
Project Management
Construction Management
Facilities Management

AFFILIATE
Wolfberg/Alvarez, CM
Construction Management

PERSONS TO CONTACT
David A. Wolfberg, AIA
Julio E. Alvarez, P.E.
Michael Konopka, AIA

REPRESENTATIVE CLIENTS
Private Clients
Avis Rent-A-Car Systems, Inc.
Burdines Department Stores
Burger King Corporation
Citicorp Savings of Florida, Inc.
Codina Development
Cordis Corporation
Emil Mosbacher Investments
Equity Properties & Development
Florida Power & Light Company
General Development Corporation
Key West Harbour Development
Liberty Real Estate Corporation
National Car Rental Systems, Inc.
National Life of Vermont
Phillips Petroleum Company
Pueblo International
Racal-Milgo Corporation
Schurgin Development Corporation
South Miami Hospital
Time-Life Books, Inc.
United Parcel Service
University of Miami
Wackenhut Systems Corporation

Public Clients
Alexandria City Public Schools, VA
Broward County, FL
City of Hialeah, FL
City of Miami, FL
City of Miami Beach, FL
Dade County School Board
Fairfax County, VA
Metropolitan-Dade County, FL
Montgomery County, MD
National Aeronautics & Space
Administration, State of Florida
U.S. Air Force
U.S. Army Corps of Engineers
U.S. Coast Guard
U.S. Department of Justice
Immigration & Naturalization Service
U.S. Department of the Treasury
Bureau of Engraving and Printing
U.S. General Services Administration
U.S. Navy
U.S. Postal Service
Veterans Administration

PROFILE
The business of Architecture is changing and Wolfberg/Alvarez & Associates is changing to meet the challenge. As part of a commitment to providing a single source of delivery and accountability, the firm has built upon an Architectural/Engineering background to provide ever expanding professional services.

Established in 1976 as a small A/E firm, Wolfberg/Alvarez & Associates became one of the most dynamic, multi-disciplined Architectural, Engineering, and Interior Design firms in the United States with a national reputation for outstanding achievement and performance. The expansion of services began in 1980 with a pioneering commitment to Computer-aided Design and Drafting (CADD) and continued through the decade with the addition of Project Management services; establishment of a Construction Management affiliate, Wolfberg/Alvarez, CM; and establishment of a Development affiliate.

The same Principals who founded Wolfberg/Alvarez & Associates continue to guide the firm's diversification and growth with an entrepreneurial approach to the business of Architecture and Engineering and an understanding of sound management practices. The initial philosophy of personal service, efficient performance, and design excellence has been maintained while achieving a balance between design and its relationship to the development of a finished product. This philosophy has resulted in the design of the broadest range of public and private facilities which are both aesthetically and financially successful.

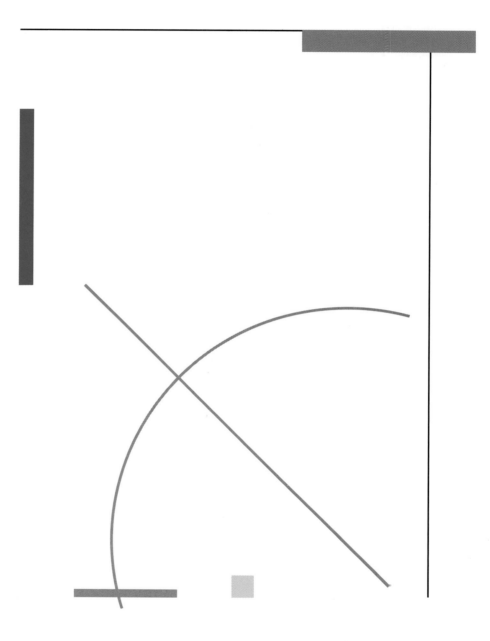

BORAL
Industries, Inc.

BORAL INDUSTRIES, INC.

BORAL INDUSTRIES, INC.

ADDRESS

800 No. Haven, Suite 240
Ontario, CA 91764

TELEPHONE

(714) 944 1700

FACSIMILE

(714) 944 1712

The Boral group of companies has become one of the world's leading suppliers of building materials and construction services. Starting in 1948, Boral refined oils for road paving in Australia and has since grown into a widely diversified organization both geographically and in services and products.

In North America, BORAL BRICKS, Inc. operates 15 widespread clay brick production facilities and 21 Boral Brick Masonry Supply Centers.

CONCRETE ROOFING TILE - Lifetile roofing tiles are produced in six automated high-volume plants located in California, Arizona, Texas and Florida.

CLAY ROOFING TILE - United States Tile Company is America's largest producer of traditional kiln-fired clay roofing tiles.

BORAL RESOURCES, Inc. operates a group of companies strategically located to serve the asphalt paving and concrete industries in southern California.

CORRUGATED METAL DRAINAGE & VENTILATION PIPE is manufactured in plants located in British Columbia and Saskatchewan provinces in Canada as well as at facilities located in Washington state and California.

FLY ASH - Western Ash Company processes fly ash from 13 western power generating stations. The product is distributed through 5 company-owned terminals - or by direct shipment to customers.

CLAY BRICK - Boral Bricks, Inc. offers the widest choice of colors, textures and shapes available in North America. Today's technologically superior clay brick, more than ever before, offers design professionals the flexibility to create truly innovative architecture.

BORAL BRICKS, Inc.,
PO Box 1957. Augusta, GA 30913

ASHE BRICK,
Van Wyck, SC (803) 286 5566

BALTIMORE BRICK,
Baltimore, MD (301) 682 6700

BORAL BRICKS LYNCHBURG,
Lynchburg, VA (804) 528 4127

BURNS BRICK,
Macon GA (912) 743 8621

DELTA BRICK,
Macon MS (601) 726 4236

GEORGIA-CAROLINA BRICK,
Augusta, GA (404) 722 6831

GLEASON BRICK,
Gleason, TN (901) 648 5429

GUIGNARD BRICK,
Columbia (Lexington), SC
(803) 3561730

HENDERSON BRICK,
Henderson, TX (214) 657 3505

MERRY BROTHERS BRICK,
Augusta, GA (404) 722 6831

OKLAHOMA BRICK,
Oklahoma City, OK (405) 946 9711

CONCRETE ROOFING TILES - Lifetile produced America's first high density, extruded concrete tiles at a plant in Fremont, California. Lifetiles are available in many styles and colors to meet any architectural design. Because they are incombustible and do not wear out when exposed to the elements, concrete tiles are America's fastest growing roofing product. Lifetile operates production facilities in California, Arizona, Texas and Florida.
BORAL CONCRETE PRODUCTS, Inc.
3511 No. Riverside Ave., Rialto, CA 92376

CLAY ROOFING TILES - Genuine kiln-fired clay roofing tiles have protected man's homes and memorable architectural wonders for centuries. Discerning architects and builders throughout the U.S. have long specified clay tiles for their natural beauty and prestige. Available in traditional 2-piece mission, "S" shape and shingle styles.
UNITED STATES TILE COMPANY,
909 Railroad Street, Corona, CA 91720

AGGREGATES & ROAD SURFACING - These Boral companies are major suppliers of asphalt surfacing products and services for the paving of highways, airports, industrial projects and residential subdivisions. Eleven hot-mixed asphalt plants and six aggregate production facilities serve the southern California market.
BORAL RESOURCES, Inc.,
15384 Arrow Highway, Fontana, CA 92335

CORRUGATED METAL DRAINAGE & VENTILATION PIPE - Galvanized steel or aluminum culverts and drain pipes are manufactured in a wide range of sizes for a variety of uses in water management including diversion, retention, spillways and erosion control. In addition to public construction projects the logging, chemical and paper industries are major customers.
CASCADE CULVERT COMPANY,
PO Box 217, Arlington, WA 98233
SPIR.L.OK INDUSTRIES CANADA, LTD,
5741 Production Way, Langley, BC V3A 4N5

FLY ASH - Western Ash Company distributes ash from coal burning power sources for use in soil stabilization and concrete construction. The company's IFA stabilizer dry bulk powder is an effective product for the treatment of waste liquids and sludges when using processes that employ stabilization - solidifications technology.
WESTERN ASH COMPANY,
50520 No. 8th Place, Phoenix, AZ 85011

1

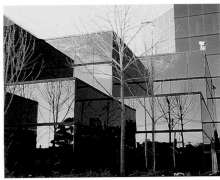

2

3

4

1. Zenith Centre, Sydney
   Austwin Units incorporating
   Suncool TS21 on green
2. Tooronga Office, Melbourne
   Suncool SS8 on grey laminate
3. Vicwood Plaza, Hong Kong
   Suncool SS8 on clear
4. Market Street Office, Melbourne
   Featuring Colourclad spandrels

PILKINGTON (AUSTRALIA) LIMITED

David Cleland   Simon de Meyrick

PILKINGTON (AUSTRALIA) LIMITED
Architectural Division

ADDRESSES

Australia
Greens Road
Dandenong, Victoria 3175
Telephone 0011 613 797 6222
Facsimile   0011 613 791 8600
Telex   AA30796

United States
Southern California
Integrated Marketing
Concepts Inc.
22632 Golden Springs Drive,
Suite 180
Diamond Bar, CA 91765
Telephone (714) 860 5000
Facsimile   (714) 861 4463

Hong Kong
McLaren Coghill Ltd.
1801 Jubilee Commercial Building
42 Gloucester Road, Hong Kong
Telephone 5-8610386
Facsimile   5-8613124
Telex   83429

New Zealand
Pilkington New Zealand Ltd.
530 Ellerslie/Panmure Highway
Panmure, Auckland 6
Telephone 0011 64 9 579 132
Facsimile   0011 64 9 579 4723
Telex   7460211

PERSONS TO CONTACT
David Cleland - General Manager
Architectural Division
Simon de Meyrick - Marketing Manager
Architectural Division
Buzz Harwood - Integrated Marketing Concepts

GLASS REFLECTING AUSTRALIA

From 1856 one of the major suppliers of window glass to Australia was the English Company, Pilkington Brothers.

In 1931, the first flat glass plant opened in Australia in competition with imports. This soon led to a close association between Australian manufacturers and Pilkington Brothers for almost 40 years which saw them eventually come together in a joint venture to produce architectural glass in 1972.

Today, Pilkington Australia is a wholly owned subsidiary of Pilkington plc. The Architectural Division is committed to assist architects and developers make the most of the enormous potential glass has to offer and to produce architectural glass to the highest quality standards.

To ensure the company's quality standards are maintained, ongoing investment is made in the latest technology and plant available. Since 1987 Pilkington Australia has invested in a new laminating line, expanded facilities for producing sputtered coatings, a new insulated glass unit line and has recently commissioned a new float plant incorporating the latest advances in glass manufacture. Technical and quality control is facilitated by all these operations being integrated and carried out on one site.

Among their quality products is the Suncool High Performance Series, which comprises a range of glasses, each with metallic oxide coating giving a distinctive appearance and high performance.

In the Suncool series there are five standard coatings available which may be applied in a range of densities to clear or tinted base glass. The resulting combinations of coatings and base glass present a broad range of color and solar control performances to suit a variety of needs.

The Suncool range is suitable for single glazing applications and is available annealed where appropriate, tempered, heat-strengthened, laminated or incorporated in sealed insulating units.

Suncool Reflective Laminated Glass combines the outstanding performance and visual appeal of Suncool High Performance Glasses with the properties and benefits of laminated glass.

Suncool Reflective Laminated Glass is characterized by:
- low visible distortion
- enhanced noise control
- safety and integrity
- ultraviolet screening
- coating protection in exposed situations
- heat and glare control

Suncool Reflective Laminated glass can be used in monolithic glazing and in insulating glass units.

Another Pilkington architectural development is Austwin Insulating Glass Units. Their primary function is to reduce air-to-air heat transfer.

Austwin units, which are a feature of the eye-catching Parliament House Building in Canberra, are extremely versatile and can be manufactured to meet different design requirements.

The main benefits of Austwin factory sealed insulating units are increased thermal insulation, improved sound insulation, greater comfort, and except in extreme circumstances, condensation is virtually eliminated.

This allows for greater use of glass in wide frontages and west facing walls which still allow buildings to remain cool - and quiet.

Pilkington Australia also has a range of four Low E coatings, including two which are reflective, for use in Austwin units. Pilkington Low E coatings can offer outstanding improvements in thermal performance with no change to aesthetics. They give fresh opportunities in design flexibility giving more options in the choice of glass.

Colourclad is another Pilkington product to prove popular with architects.

A ceramic coated, heat-strengthened/tempered glass, it is a virtually maintenance free cladding material because the coating is permanently fused to the inside surface of the glass.

The main use for Colourclad is for infill or spandrel panels in curtain wall construction where an opaque area is required, but still retaining the surface integrity of the glazing.

Colourclad is a decorated glass product with all the advantages of glass together with the designer options of color and form.

Colourback is the superior choice for cost efficient spanderel glass or cladding panels wherever an attractive finish is needed.

It offers architects and interior designers the opportunity to create a unique but practical element to exterior and interior applications.

With Colourback overall color, bends, lines, grid and dot patterns can be incorporated to complement building detail.

Architectural glass technology is certainly of the fastest expanding fields in the building and construction industries.

To meet the challenges being asked of architectural glass, Pilkington has developed its Technical Service Group, which is staffed by qualified engineers who are experts in their own field. One of the primary ways in which they assist architects is by employing highly specialized computer programs to compare, with great accuracy, potential and proposed glazing alternatives. These alternatives increasingly involve environmental and structural design applications, including thermal and structural loading, glasses for solar control and glasses capable of withstanding human and missile impact.

THE WOOL BUREAU, INC.

With qualifications like extraordinary beauty, luxuriant texture, rich patina and exceptional performance, it's no wonder wool is the natural choice of specifiers. For corporate, hospitality, health care and store planning, wool handles heavy traffic head-on.

Offering a wide variety of products, immediate availability and custom possibilities, wool can meet all project specifications, large or small.

The Wool Bureau, Inc.
Interior Textile Division
240 Peachtree Street, N.W.
Merchandise Mart
Space 6F-11
Atlanta, GA 30303-1301
Telephone (404) 524 0512

Executive Offices
360 Lexington Avenue
New York, NY 10017-6572
Telephone (212) 986 6222

Designers/Manufacturers (L-R):
Bianca Quantrell for Kaleidoscope, Shaw Commercial Systems; David Cadwallader for Schumacher Contract, Collins & Aikman; Charles E. Pavarini for Scalamandré, Bloomsburg Carpets.

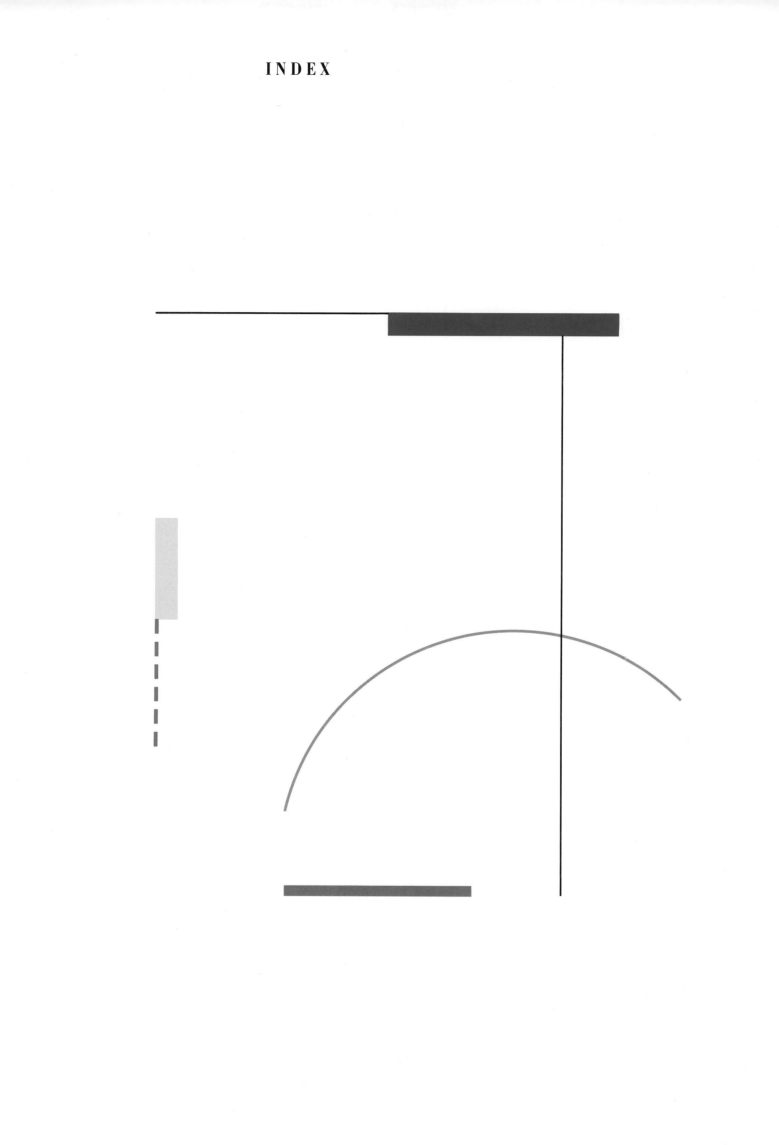

NAME OF PRACTICE

		REGIONS OF SERVICES									PROJECT TYPES											
Name of Practice	Page Number	North America	South America	Europe/North Atlantic	Africa	Middle East	Northern Asia	East Asia	South East Asia	Oceania	Aged Care	Civic	Commercial	Ecclesiastical	Educational	Health/Laboratories	Industrial	Interior Design	Landscape	Recreation/Refurbishment	Town Planning	Other
ADACHE ASSOCIATES ARCHITECTS, P.A.	14-15	•																•		•		Hotel & Resort
AEPA	16-17	•	•	•		•	•	•	•	•				•	•			•				
ALBERT C. MARTIN AND ASSOCIATES	18-19	•					•	•						•	•	•	•	•			*	• * Urban Design; Building, Engineering Renovation/Retrofit Criminal Justice
BOHLIN POWELL LARKIN CYWINSKI	20-21	•										•	•	•	•	•	•	•	•	•	•	
JOHN BURGEE ARCHITECTS	22-23	•	•	•	•	•	•	•	•	•		•	•	•	•							Cultural Mixed-Use Residential
CAMBRIDGE SEVEN ASSOCIATES, INC.	24-25	•						•	•	•		•	•		•	•				•	•	
CBT/CHILDS BERTMAN TSECKARES & CASENDINO INC.	26-27	•	•		•							•	•		•			•	•	•	•	Urban Design
CHAIX & JOHNSON INTERNATIONAL, INC.	28-29	•	•					•	•	•			•		•			•		•	•	
CLARK HOLMAN & MOORHEAD, LTD.	30-31	•									•	•	•	•	•			•				Residential/Housing
COOPER CARRY & ASSOCIATES, INC.	32-33	•											•		•			•	•			Master Planning

NAME OF PRACTICE	PAGE NUMBER	REGIONS OF SERVICES									PROJECT TYPES											OTHER
		NORTH AMERICA	SOUTH AMERICA	EUROPE/NORTH ATLANTIC	AFRICA	MIDDLE EAST	NORTHERN ASIA	EAST ASIA	SOUTH EAST ASIA	OCEANIA	AGED CARE	CIVIC	COMMERCIAL	ECCLESIASTICAL	EDUCATIONAL	HEALTH/LABORATORIES	INDUSTRIAL	INTERIOR DESIGN	LANDSCAPE	RECREATION/REFURBISHMENT	TOWN PLANNING	
COOPER•LECKY	34-35	•		•							•	•	•	•	•			•		•		
LEO A DALY	36-37	•	•	•	•	•	•	•	•	•	•	•	•	•	•	•	•	•		•		Air Transportation Facilities
DAN PETER KOPPLE & ASSOCIATES	38-39	•		•									*		•					•	•	* Offices Parking Facilities Development Consulting Transportation Facilities
DELAWIE/BRETTON/ WILKES ASSOCIATES	40-41	•				•					•	•		•	•	•		•	•	•	•	Aquariums and Aquatic Parks
DEMAREST & ASSOCIATES ARCHITECTS, INC.	42-43	•									•	•						•	•			Multi-family Housing
DESIGN PARTNERS INCORPORATED	44-45	•						•	•		•	•	•	•	•	•	•	•		•		
DWL ARCHITECTS + PLANNERS, INC.	46-47	•		•									•		•	•	•	•				
DWORSKY ASSOCIATES, ARCHITECTS & PLANNERS	48-49	•						•		•	•	•		•	•		•		•		Correctional/Institutional
ELLERBE BECKET	50-51	•				•	•	•	•		•		•		•			•		•	•	Hospitality Passenger Cruise Vessels Airport/Airline Terminals
ELLIOTT + ASSOCIATES ARCHITECTS	52-53	•									•	•						•				Renovation/Restoration

NAME OF PRACTICE	PAGE NUMBER	REGIONS OF SERVICES									PROJECT TYPES											OTHER
		NORTH AMERICA	SOUTH AMERICA	EUROPE/NORTH ATLANTIC	AFRICA	MIDDLE EAST	NORTHERN ASIA	EAST ASIA	SOUTH EAST ASIA	OCEANIA	AGED CARE	CIVIC	COMMERCIAL	ECCLESIASTICAL	EDUCATIONAL	HEALTH/LABORATORIES	INDUSTRIAL	INTERIOR DESIGN	LANDSCAPE	RECREATION/REFURBISHMENT	TOWN PLANNING	
EARL R. FLANSBURGH + ASSOCIATES, INC.	54-55	•	•	•						•	•	•	•		•	•		•	•	•		
FRANKFURT-SHORT-BRUZA ASSOCIATES, P.C.	56-57	•											•	•		•	•	•	•	•		
FRANK O. GEHRY & ASSOCIATES	58-59	•		•									•	•		•	•			•		
GOULD EVANS ARCHITECTS, P.A.	60-61	•											•	•	•	•		•		•		Retail, Restoration, Residential, Master Planning, Libraries, Government
GRAHAM GUND ARCHITECTS	62-63	•											•		•			•			•	Museums/ Performing Arts, Historic Preservation, Rehab/Renovations, Urban Planning Design
MICHAEL GRAVES, ARCHITECT	64-65	•	•	•			•	•		•		•	•	•	•			•		•	•	Museums, Libraries
GROUP 70 LIMITED	66-67	•					•	•	•			•			•			•			•	Resort Planning, Hotels, Housing
HANSEN LIND MEYER INC.	68-69	•										•	•	•	•	•	•	•	•	•	•	Judicial & Courtroom Facilities, Prison & Correctional Facilities
HARDY HOLZMAN PFEIFFER ASSOCIATES	70-71	•										•	•*	•	•	•		•		•	•**	* Corporate ** Urban Development Restoration, Renovation and Re-use
HARPER CARRENO INC. SHWC HARPER CARRENO INC.	72-73	•									•	•	•	•	•	•	•	•	•	•	•	Justice

NAME OF PRACTICE	PAGE NUMBER	REGIONS OF SERVICES									PROJECT TYPES											OTHER
		NORTH AMERICA	SOUTH AMERICA	EUROPE/NORTH ATLANTIC	AFRICA	MIDDLE EAST	NORTHERN ASIA	EAST ASIA	SOUTH EAST ASIA	OCEANIA	AGED CARE	CIVIC	COMMERCIAL	ECCLESIASTICAL	EDUCATIONAL	HEALTH/LABORATORIES	INDUSTRIAL	INTERIOR DESIGN	LANDSCAPE	RECREATION/REFURBISHMENT	TOWN PLANNING	
HELLMUTH, OBATA & KASSABAUM, INC.	74-75	•	•	•	•	•	•	•	•	•	•	•	•	•	•	•	•	•	•	•	•	Criminal Justice Retail; Mixed Use
HKS INC.	76-77	•	•	•		•		•	•	•	*	•	•	•	•	•	•	•			•	* Extended Care Correctional, Housing
HOWARD NEEDLES TAMMEN & BERGENDOFF	78-79	•								•		•	•		•	•	•	•	•	•	•	Airport Terminals, Sports Facilities, Historic Preservation
THE JERDE PARTNERSHIP INC.	80-81	•	•	•		•		•		•		•	•		•					•	•	Urban Planning
JOHNSON FAIN AND PEREIRA ASSOCIATES	82-83	•	•	•		•		•	•	•			*		•		•	•			•	* Office Retail Residential Urban Design & Planning Governmental
JPJ ARCHITECTS, INC.	84-85	•								•	•	•	•	•	•	•		•				Hotels Computer Centers
KEYS CONDON FLORANCE ARCHITECTS	86-87	•										•	•		•	•		•	•	•	•	Renovation & Restoration Corporate
KOHN PEDERSEN FOX ASSOCIATES, P.C.	88-89	•						•	•			•	•		•			•				
LANGDON WILSON ARCHITECTS PLANNERS	90-91	•					•					•			•	•	•	•		•	•	Cultural Hotel/Resort
LAWTON & UMEMURA, ARCHITECTS, AIA, INC.	92-93	•	•						•	•	•	•	•	•	•		•	•		•	•	Retail Resort/Hospitality

NAME OF PRACTICE	PAGE NUMBER	NORTH AMERICA	SOUTH AMERICA	EUROPE/NORTH ATLANTIC	AFRICA	MIDDLE EAST	NORTHERN ASIA	EAST ASIA	SOUTH EAST ASIA	OCEANIA	AGED CARE	CIVIC	COMMERCIAL	ECCLESIASTICAL	EDUCATIONAL	HEALTH/LABORATORIES	INDUSTRIAL	INTERIOR DESIGN	LANDSCAPE	RECREATION/REFURBISHMENT	TOWN PLANNING	OTHER
LEASON POMEROY ASSOCIATES, INC.	94-95	•					•				•	•	•		•		•	•	•	•	•	Retail
THE LUCKMAN PARTNERSHIP, INC	96-97	•											•	•	•	•	•	•		•		Hotels Sports Facilities Convention Centers
MACLACHLAN, CORNELIUS & FILONI, ARCHITECTS, INC.	98-99	•												•	•	•	•	•		•	• *	* Urban Planning Theaters
MARIANI & ASSOCIATES	100-101	•	•	•	•	•							•		•	•	•	•				Historic Preservation Pre-fabrication
MARTINEZ/WONG & ASSOCIATES, INC.	102-103	•	•					•	•				•	•	•			•	•		•	
MEDIA FIVE LIMITED	104-105	•						•	•	•		•	•	•		•	•		•		•	•	Graphic Design Hotel & Resort Residential
RICHARD MEIER & PARTNERS	106-107	•	•	•	•	•	•	•	•	•			•	•	•	•	•	•	•			•	Residential Cultural - Museums
MITCHELL/GIURGOLA ARCHITECTS NEW YORK	108-109	•	•	•		•	•	•	•	•				•		•	•	•	•		•	•	Cultural & Exhibition Theaters, Concert Halls
MURPHY/JAHN	110-111	•	•	•	•	•	•	•	•	•			• *	•		•		•	•				* Institutional Transportation/Airports Exhibition Sports Facilities Mixed Use, Office, Hotel, Multi-family Residential
NACHT & LEWIS ARCHITECTS, INC.	112-113	•											•	•		•	•	•	•		•	

NAME OF PRACTICE	PAGE NUMBER	REGIONS OF SERVICES									PROJECT TYPES											
		NORTH AMERICA	SOUTH AMERICA	EUROPE/NORTH ATLANTIC	AFRICA	MIDDLE EAST	NORTHERN ASIA	EAST ASIA	SOUTH EAST ASIA	OCEANIA	AGED CARE	CIVIC	COMMERCIAL	ECCLESIASTICAL	EDUCATIONAL	HEALTH/LABORATORIES	INDUSTRIAL	INTERIOR DESIGN	LANDSCAPE	RECREATION/REFURBISHMENT	TOWN PLANNING	OTHER
NBBJ	114-115	•		•			•	•	•	•	•	•		•	•	•	•	•	•	•	•	
PFLUEGER ARCHITECTS, INC.	116-117	•	•	•			•	•	•	•	•	•		•	•	•		•		•	•	Energy Studies Programming Housing
ROYSTON HANAMOTO ALLEY & ABEY	118-119	•	•	•				•	•	•		•		•		•			•	•	•	Cemeteries Housing Resorts
RTKL	120-121	•	•	•	•	•	•	•	•	•	•	•		•	•	•	•	•	•	•	•	
SANDY & BABCOCK INC	122-123	•					•	•		•		•		•								Resort, Hotel, Multi-family, Master Planning
SKIDMORE, OWINGS & MERRILL	124-125	•	•	•	•	•	•	•	•	•	•	•		•	•	•	•	•	•	•	•	Airports, Race Courses, Stadia, Libraries, Museums, Mixed Use, Residential, Hotels, Subway and Train Stations, Retail
SPRANKLE, LYND & SPRAGUE, ARCHITECTS	126-127	•	•				•	•	•	•		•		•	•		•	•	•			
ROBERT A.M. STERN ARCHITECTS	128-129	•	•				•	•	•	•	•	•	•	•		•	•	•		*	•	* Urban Design Decorative Arts Hotels
WILLIAM B. TABLER ARCHITECTS	130-131	•	•	•		•	•	•	•	•			•		•					•		Hotels & Resorts Conference Centers
THE STUBBINS ASSOCIATES, INC.	132-133	•	•	•		•		•	•				•		•	•		•	•	•		Master Planning Signage

		REGIONS OF SERVICES									PROJECT TYPES											
NAME OF PRACTICE	PAGE NUMBER	NORTH AMERICA	SOUTH AMERICA	EUROPE/NORTH ATLANTIC	AFRICA	MIDDLE EAST	NORTHERN ASIA	EAST ASIA	SOUTH EAST ASIA	OCEANIA	AGED CARE	CIVIC	COMMERCIAL	ECCLESIASTICAL	EDUCATIONAL	HEALTH/LABORATORIES	INDUSTRIAL	INTERIOR DESIGN	LANDSCAPE	RECREATION/REFURBISHMENT	TOWN PLANNING	OTHER
THREE	134-135	●	●	●				●	●	●			●					●			●	Master Planning Residential
UELAND AND JUNKER ARCHITECTS AND PLANNERS	136-137	●	●									●	●	●	●	●		●			●	Exhibit Design Museums
WIMBERLY ALLISON TONG & GOO	138-139	●		●		●	●	●	●	●			●		●					●	●*	* Master, Site, Transportation, Resort, Waterfront Theaters, Mixed Use, Hotels/Resorts, Clubs, Military
THE WISCHMEYER ARCHITECTS	140-141	●									●	●	●	●	●	●	●	●	●	*●		* Renovation
WOLFBERG/ALVAREZ & ASSOCIATES	142-143	●	●	●							●	●	●		●	●	●	●				
WOODFORD PARKINSON WYNN & PARTNERS, ARCHITECTS	144-145	●									●	●	●		●	●	●	●		●		Preservation Aviation High tech/Computer Facilites

U.S.A. STATE ABBREVIATIONS

Alaska	AK	Montana	MT
Alabama	AL	North Carolina	NC
Arkansas	AR	North Dakota	ND
Arizona	AZ	Nebraska	NE
California	CA	New Hampshire	NH
Colorado	CO	New Jersey	NJ
Connecticut	CT	New Mexico	NM
District of Columbia	DC	Nevada	NV
Delaware	DE	New York	NY
Florida	FL	Ohio	OH
Georgia	GA	Oklahoma	OK
Guam	GU	Oregon	OR
Hawaii	HI	Pennsylvania	PA
Iowa	IA	Puerto Rico	PR
Idaho	ID	Rhode Island	RI
Illinois	IL	South Carolina	SC
Indiana	IN	South Dakota	SD
Kansas	KS	Tennessee	TN
Kentucky	KY	Texas	TX
Louisiana	LA	Utah	UT
Massachusetts	MA	Virginia	VA
Maryland	MD	Virgin Islands	VI
Maine	ME	Vermont	VT
Michigan	MI	Washington	WA
Minnesota	MN	Wisconsin	WI
Missouri	MO	West Virginia	WV
Mississippi	MS	Wyoming	WY

THE IMAGES PUBLISHING GROUP

Directors: (L-R):
Paul Latham and Alessina Brooks

**THE IMAGES PUBLISHING
GROUP**
Publishing Marketing

ESTABLISHED DATE
1983

ADDRESS
Images House
6 Bastow Place
Mulgrave, Victoria 3170
Australia

TELEPHONE
(613) 561 5544

FACSIMILE
(613) 561 4860

DIRECTORS
Paul A. Latham
Alessina R. Brooks

PERSONS TO CONTACT
Either Director

PROJECT TYPES
Publishers
Market Research
Promotional Material
Graphic Design

The Images Publishing Group is a Division of Images Australia Pty Ltd. Its formation is part of an international initiative by the parent company to steadily expand its operations, and its reputation for works of excellence, into each of the major economic regions of the world. We are succeeding in this endeavour and this year won Australia's coveted National Print Award Silver Medal.

Like all of its companion volumes, "Architects of the United States of America" is not a directory. If it were, the participants would no doubt have numbered in their thousands and the overall standard of entries would have been predictably mediocre.

Instead, what we have sought to produce in this present work is an unique and current portrayal of the "cream" of American Architects and their Architecture. It is a demonstration of their very finest creative achievements and the highest standards of professionalism which underpin their expertise in the world of building design and construction.

Our principal objectives in doing this are threefold:

• to make this remarkable volume the leading and most sought after reference source within the construction and development market in North America and elsewhere.

• to provide a previously unavailable opportunity for American Architects to share in the promotional benefits flowing from the distribution of presentation copies of this volume to the Images list of several thousand key decision makers in public and private sectors around the world.

• to facilitate the expansion of an outstanding network of collaborative linkages between the large and growing range of professionals now participating in The Images Profile Series, and, through such affiliations help to build international project teams of the highest competitive standard.

Another vital part of The Images Publishing Group's marketing strategy is to ensure that the publication is widely available for sale in leading bookshops throughout North America.

Overall, our experience shows that there is a growing interest in and demand for world-class specialist reference volumes. However, it is clear that without the exceptionally high quality of each one of the entries, the public interest, demand and marketing potential of The Images Profile Series would not be nearly so significant.

It is a great privilege for The Images Publishing Group to have worked with the Architects of the United States of America to produce a book of such striking character and enduring quality. We therefore wish to thank, most sincerely, each of the participants for providing material of such high standard as to make this book and its contents an unequivocal benchmark of excellence and success.

CREDITS

Published by
The Images Publishing Group
Images House
6 Bastow Place
Mulgrave, Victoria 3170
Australia
Telephone   (613) 561 5544
Facsimile   (613) 561 4860
Designed by
Russell Bevers Design Pty Ltd
Color Separations by
Enticott
Printed by
Owen King Printers Australia Pty Ltd

The information and illustrations in this publication have been prepared and supplied by the entrants. While all reasonable efforts have been made to ensure accuracy, the publishers do not, under any circumstances, accept responsibility for errors, omissions and representations express or implied.